Volume 3 of the Empire Blueprint Series: Case Studies for Business Success

74 Case Studies in Growth, Digital Presence, and Legacy Building

ALSO BY AUTHORSDOOR GROUP

Empire Builders Series: Masterclasses in Business and Law
Expert Insights Into Business Strategy and Legal Acumen

Brick by Brick: The Entrepreneur's Guide to Constructing a Company

Mark Your Territory: Navigating Trademarks in the Modern Marketplace

From Idea to Empire: Mastering the Art of Business Planning

From Idea to Empire: Abridged Edition

Beyond the Pen: Copyright Strategies for Modern Creators

Legal Ink: Navigating the Legalese of Publishing

The Empire Blueprint Series: Case Studies for Business Success
Strategies to Grow, Innovate, and Leave a Lasting Legacy

70 Case Studies in Vision, Strategy, and Personal Branding

70 Case Studies in Leadership, Innovation, and Resilience

74 Case Studies in Growth, Digital presence, and Legacy Building

AuthorsDoor Series: *Publisher & Her World*
The Surprisingly Simple Truth Behind Extraordinary Results

AuthorsDoor Advanced Series: *Publisher & Her World*
Adventures in Publishing and the Creation of Super Brands

AuthorsDoor Masterclass Series: *Publisher & Her World*
The Essential Keys to Unlocking Unstoppable Growth

Volume 3 of the Empire Blueprint Series: Case Studies for
Business Success

---

74 Case Studies in Growth, Digital Presence, and Legacy Building

Strategies for Long-Term Success

L. A. MOESZINGER

AuthorsDoor Group
an imprint of The Ridge Publishing Group

Library of Congress Control Number: 2024922969

74 Case Studies in Growth, Digital Presence, and Legacy Building: Strategies for Long-Term Success / by L. A. Moeszinger

ISBN 978-1-956905-43-4 (e-book)
ISBN 978-1-956905-42-7 (softcover)

1. Business & Economics / Entrepreneurship. 2. Business & Economics / Small Business. 3. Business & Economics / Management. 4. Self-Help / Motivational & Inspiration. 5. Business & Economics / Leadership. I. Title. II. Series

Printed in the United States of America

Dedicated to the trailblazers and builders whose relentless pursuit of growth, mastery of digital presence, and commitment to legacy inspire future generations to dream bigger.

AuthorsDoor Group
Coeur d'Alene, Idaho

INTRODUCTION.TO THE
AUTHORSDOOR LEADERSHIP PROGRAM

The AuthorsDoor Leadership Program, separate from the Builders Empire Series, is a new initiative designed to empower authors and publishers with the skills to effectively sell books. It features three tailored series: (1) AuthorsDoor Series: *Publisher & Her World*, (2) AuthorsDoor Advanced Series: *Publisher & Her World*, and (3) AuthorsDoor Masterclass Series: *Publisher & Her World*; each series is meticulously structured to guide participants from foundational concepts to advanced strategies in selling books, book by book, in a chronological format. The courses, offered for free on our YouTube channels—Publisher & Her World at Ridge Publishing Group, AuthorsDoor Group: Publisher & Her World, and Authors Red Door #Shorts—complement the books and workbooks, each providing unique and valuable teachings.

Explore additional resources to enhance your journey:

- Follow our blog at AuthorsRedDoor.com.
- Subscribe to our Newsletters at AuthorsDoor.com.
- Join our AuthorsDoor Strategy Forum Facebook Group.
- Connect with our Facebook Page at AuthorsDoor Group.
- Become a fan on our social media channels @AuthorsDoor1.

For feedback or questions, contact us at info@authorsdoor.com. We are here to support your journey from writing to successfully selling your books.

Warm regards,

L. A. Moeszinger #PubHerWorld

Contents

Introduction

74 Case Studies in Growth, Digital Presence, and Legacy Building

In the modern business landscape, achieving long-term success requires more than just hitting short-term goals—it demands a combination of vision, strategic growth, strong digital presence, and the creation of a lasting legacy. Volume 3 of the Empire Blueprint Series brings together 74 real-world case studies that dive deep into the critical elements of business expansion, brand development, storytelling, and innovation. Through these stories, readers gain insight into the processes and strategies that distinguish thriving enterprises from those that merely survive.

Whether you're starting a business, scaling operations, or enhancing your digital presence, this book offers actionable frameworks for building sustainable growth. Each case study reveals how leaders shape visions, craft meaningful stories, and harness digital platforms to create impact—and how they align these efforts with the ultimate goal of leaving a legacy that extends beyond profit. This volume is not just a guide; it's a toolkit for anyone seeking to build something enduring, innovative, and deeply impactful.

Shaping a Vision That Drives Growth

At the heart of every great enterprise lies a vision that inspires and motivates action. The first section of this volume explores how leaders cultivate clear, compelling visions that serve as roadmaps for their business journeys. Readers will learn how to align strategic goals with that vision, ensuring that every action contributes to long-term growth. These case studies also highlight the importance of flexibility—allowing businesses to adapt and refine their vision as circumstances change.

Turning Goals into Reality Through Strong Frameworks

Vision alone isn't enough—execution is where ideas come to life. This section focuses on practical frameworks for business growth, detailing how companies move from planning to action. It covers essential strategies such as resource management, operational scalability, and time leadership. Readers will also explore how efficiency tools and processes help leaders make the most of their time, ensuring that growth is both sustainable and strategic.

Developing a Brand That Stands Out in Crowded Markets

In today's competitive landscape, a distinctive brand can make the difference between success and obscurity. This volume emphasizes the art of branding, offering real-world examples of how businesses define their unique identities and communicate them effectively. From logos and messaging to customer experiences, these case studies show how strong branding builds recognition, trust, and loyalty—ultimately laying the foundation for long-term success.

Mastering Storytelling and Expanding Reach Online

Effective marketing today goes beyond traditional advertising—it's about storytelling that resonates with audiences. This section reveals how businesses use narratives to captivate customers, communicate their missions, and differentiate themselves in saturated markets. Readers will also learn how to expand their reach through digital communities and social media platforms, gaining insights into building authentic connections and meaningful engagement with audiences worldwide.

Leveraging Innovation for Continuous Expansion

Innovation is not a one-time event—it's an ongoing process that fuels growth. The case studies in this section explore how leaders foster a culture of innovation within their organizations, using it as a tool for business expansion and long-term sustainability. Readers will discover strategies for developing new products, improving processes, and entering new markets, ensuring their businesses stay relevant and competitive.

Navigating the Social Media Landscape for Brand Growth

Social media has become one of the most powerful tools for building brand awareness and driving customer engagement. This volume provides insights into navigating social platforms strategically, showing how businesses leverage different channels to connect with diverse audiences, grow communities, and promote products. The case studies also explore best practices for managing content, campaigns, and engagement metrics, ensuring that businesses maximize the impact of their online presence.

Driving Impactful Legacy-Building Strategies

The final section focuses on the importance of legacy creation, offering readers insights into how businesses align day-to-day operations with long-term goals. These case studies reveal how organizations embed purpose and values into their growth strategies, ensuring that their efforts create meaningful impact beyond financial success. Whether through philanthropy, community involvement, or sustainable practices, readers will discover how leaders leave behind legacies that endure for generations.

Practical Insights and Tools for Long-Term Success

This book provides not only inspiring case studies but also practical tools for integrating the lessons into your own business or career. Whether you're an entrepreneur, business leader, marketer, or strategist, the strategies shared in this volume offer real-world solutions for building a business that adapts, grows, and leaves a lasting impact.

Volume 3 serves as both a roadmap and a companion, guiding readers to balance immediate goals with future vision and navigate the complexities of digital presence and brand identity. With each case study, readers will gain actionable insights on how to drive innovation, grow strategically, and create legacies that stand the test of time.

This volume is not just about achieving growth—it's about building businesses that matter, resonate, and endure. Whether you are starting fresh or looking to take your business to the next level, the lessons from these 74 case studies will empower you to align your digital presence, personal leadership, and brand identity with your long-term vision. Use this book as a tool to unlock new opportunities, inspire your team, and build something that truly lasts.

A Focus on Balance Between Growth and Sustainability

Achieving long-term business success requires more than rapid growth—it demands sustainable practices that ensure the organization's stability and adaptability over time. Many businesses succeed in scaling quickly, but the real challenge lies in building a foundation that balances short-term success with long-term sustainability. This section explores how leaders strategically align their growth ambitions with responsible business practices, ensuring their enterprises thrive without exhausting resources or compromising future potential.

Sustainable growth involves developing frameworks that support consistent, healthy expansion without overextending finances, operations, or human capital. The case studies in this volume highlight the importance of measured scaling, showing how businesses that grow too fast without strategic foresight often encounter operational bottlenecks, cash flow issues, or cultural erosion. On the other hand, those that take deliberate steps to build capacity—such as investing in technology, training employees, or refining workflows—are better positioned to navigate challenges while maintaining stability.

Another critical element of sustainable growth is customer engagement and retention. Companies highlighted in this section demonstrate that success lies not just in acquiring new customers but in nurturing long-term relationships through meaningful interactions and value-driven service. These leaders build customer trust and loyalty, turning satisfied buyers into brand advocates who support the company's growth organically.

Sustainability also extends to employee well-being and corporate culture. Leaders must ensure that the pace of growth does not outstrip the organization's ability to support its workforce, both financially and emotionally. The case studies show how businesses that prioritize employee development, mental health, and work-life balance foster more engaged teams, reducing turnover and boosting productivity. By aligning employee needs with business objectives, companies ensure that their internal structures grow as steadily as their external achievements.

Environmental sustainability is another essential focus for modern enterprises. Many of the businesses featured have incorporated eco-conscious strategies—from energy-efficient operations to responsible sourcing—into their growth plans. These companies recognize that sustainable practices not only protect the planet but also resonate with today's consumers, who increasingly prefer to support businesses aligned with their values.

Ultimately, balancing growth with sustainability requires a long-term mindset. Successful leaders embrace growth opportunities but also ensure that their strategies are scalable and adaptable over time. This section offers valuable insights into how businesses develop flexible models, maintain operational health, and align growth with social responsibility—creating enterprises that thrive in both the short and long term.

Practical Application of Digital Tools

In today's connected world, digital tools are essential for building, expanding, and sustaining business success. From automation to analytics, leveraging the right technologies can enhance productivity, streamline processes, and engage customers more effectively. This section explores how businesses and leaders use specific digital tools to boost efficiency, improve marketing efforts, and support long-term growth.

A critical focus in the case studies is the role of data analytics. Companies use data to gain real-time insights into customer behavior, market trends, and internal performance metrics, allowing them to make informed decisions. Analytics tools like Google Analytics and business intelligence software empower leaders to measure KPIs, optimize campaigns, and identify new opportunities for growth. These data-driven approaches enable organizations to react quickly to changes and maintain a competitive edge.

Another area of importance is digital marketing platforms. The case studies highlight how companies strategically use email marketing tools, social media schedulers, and CRM systems to build brand awareness, nurture leads, and engage customers at various touchpoints. Email campaigns powered by automation tools ensure timely, personalized communication, while social media platforms provide opportunities to connect with audiences, build communities, and foster loyalty.

Project management and collaboration tools also play a significant role in fostering teamwork and maintaining operational efficiency. Businesses featured in this section use tools like Trello, Asana, and Slack to organize tasks, improve communication, and streamline workflows—whether for remote or on-site teams. By creating transparent, collaborative environments, these tools help leaders manage time and resources effectively.

Additionally, e-commerce platforms and SEO optimization tools allow businesses to expand their reach and grow revenue streams. Companies optimize their websites through SEO techniques, ensuring higher visibility on search engines, while e-commerce integrations provide customers with seamless purchasing experiences. These tools are especially vital for businesses aiming to scale operations globally or tap into online markets.

The key takeaway from this section is that digital tools must be strategically integrated into business processes to deliver meaningful results. The companies profiled illustrate that it's not about adopting every new tool but about choosing the right ones aligned with their goals and operational needs. By embracing digital transformation thoughtfully, businesses enhance both internal productivity and external impact, setting the stage for sustainable growth in an increasingly digital world.

Personal Growth and Leadership Development in a Digital World

In a world where technology evolves rapidly, leadership development requires a blend of personal growth and digital fluency. Leaders today must navigate both personal challenges and professional demands, balancing their individual development with the fast-paced dynamics of the digital era. This section explores how leaders cultivate self-awareness, emotional intelligence, and adaptability, allowing them to thrive in increasingly complex environments.

The case studies demonstrate that effective leadership goes beyond managing teams—it starts with personal mastery. Leaders must develop discipline, resilience, and mental clarity to handle pressure and uncertainty. This often involves honing time management techniques, adopting practices like mindfulness and reflective thinking, and building healthy routines to maintain focus and well-being.

In the digital age, leadership also demands upskilling and continuous learning. Leaders must stay current with emerging technologies, digital tools, and market trends to make informed decisions. The case studies highlight how forward-thinking leaders invest in learning platforms, webinars, and mentorship programs to refine their technical and soft skills. This commitment to learning not only improves personal growth but also inspires teams to follow suit.

Digital communication skills are equally essential for leaders to connect with employees and customers. Remote work environments, virtual collaboration tools, and online communities require leaders to master digital presence and communication platforms like Zoom, Slack, and LinkedIn. Effective leaders use these tools to foster transparent and engaging communication, building trust and cohesion among dispersed teams.

Personal growth in a digital world also means developing empathy and emotional intelligence—skills that enable leaders to motivate others, manage conflicts, and create inclusive cultures. The case studies reveal how leaders who exhibit self-awareness and empathy cultivate stronger relationships and higher levels of employee engagement, especially in remote and hybrid work environments.

Ultimately, the digital world demands leaders who are adaptive, agile, and grounded. They must learn to balance their personal development with professional growth, embracing both technological tools and emotional intelligence to lead effectively. This section provides valuable insights into how today's leaders evolve continuously, inspire innovation, and create meaningful impact by growing as individuals while navigating the complexities of the digital landscape.

The Power of Community and Collaborative Growth

Successful businesses no longer operate in isolation—collaborative growth and community-building are essential components of long-term success. In an interconnected world, leaders who embrace collaboration—both within their organizations and across industries—achieve greater impact by leveraging diverse skills, perspectives, and shared goals. This section explores how businesses foster internal teamwork, build strategic partnerships, and engage digital communities to fuel sustainable growth.

Internally, collaborative growth begins with creating inclusive cultures that promote teamwork and shared ownership. The case studies highlight how effective leaders empower employees, fostering environments where team members feel valued, motivated, and connected to the company's mission. These companies use collaboration tools like Slack, Microsoft Teams, and Asana to streamline communication, ensuring employees can work efficiently across departments and locations. Leaders who cultivate psychological safety—where employees feel comfortable sharing ideas without fear of judgment—drive innovation and strengthen their workforce.

Externally, businesses grow by forging partnerships with other organizations—from strategic alliances and joint ventures to influencer collaborations. These partnerships allow companies to enter new markets, share resources, and combine expertise for mutual benefit. Many case studies reveal how businesses engage with suppliers, industry associations, and academic institutions to develop innovative solutions and stay competitive in evolving markets.

Digital platforms offer unprecedented opportunities for community engagement. Companies that build online communities around their brands—whether through social media, forums, or niche networks—create loyal customer bases that drive growth through word-of-mouth advocacy. The case studies show how leaders leverage social listening tools, virtual events, and user-generated content to deepen relationships and foster brand loyalty.

Community-building also extends to corporate social responsibility (CSR) initiatives. Businesses that align their values with social causes create meaningful impact while enhancing their brand reputation. This section highlights examples of companies that support local communities, engage in environmental initiatives, and create programs that align with customer interests, turning community engagement into a strategic advantage.

In essence, the power of collaboration and community lies in shared growth. Businesses that embrace collaboration foster innovative solutions, deeper connections, and more sustainable growth. Whether through internal teamwork, strategic partnerships, or community involvement, these enterprises thrive by harnessing the collective strength of their networks—proving that success is strongest when shared.

The Role of Innovation in Preventing Plateau

One of the most significant challenges businesses face is the plateau effect—a point where growth stagnates despite previous successes. In fast-moving markets, staying static means falling behind. The key to avoiding stagnation is continuous innovation. This section explores how businesses across industries use creative thinking, experimentation, and disruptive strategies to push past plateaus and unlock new avenues for growth.

Innovation doesn't have to be radical—small, incremental improvements can create compounding benefits over time. Companies highlighted in these case studies adopt process innovations that improve efficiency, reduce costs, and boost productivity. For example, businesses leverage automation and AI tools to streamline operations and free up resources for higher-value activities. By fostering a culture of continuous improvement, these organizations ensure they stay agile and ready to adapt to changing conditions.

In many cases, innovation means reimagining customer experiences to meet evolving expectations. The case studies show how companies introduce new products, services, or delivery models to remain relevant. Some businesses pivot into new markets or launch digital offerings, finding untapped opportunities that align with changing consumer behavior. Leaders also use design thinking and agile methodologies to experiment quickly, gather feedback, and make improvements—ensuring that innovations are always customer-focused.

A key lesson from these case studies is the importance of cultivating a culture of experimentation. Companies that encourage employees to take risks, explore new ideas, and embrace failure as part of the learning process develop innovation ecosystems that fuel long-term growth. Leaders provide resources, autonomy, and incentives for teams to explore new possibilities, knowing that breakthroughs often arise from unexpected places.

Technology plays a crucial role in driving innovation, from AI and data analytics to blockchain and IoT solutions. These tools enable businesses to automate processes, enhance personalization, and predict trends, giving them a competitive advantage. The companies featured in these case studies understand that innovation is not a one-time event—it's a continuous journey that requires commitment, curiosity, and adaptability.

Ultimately, the organizations that innovate consistently and strategically are the ones that not only survive plateaus but use them as springboards for further growth. This section emphasizes that innovation is not just about staying ahead— it's about staying in the game, ensuring your business remains relevant, resilient, and ready for the future.

Strategic Legacy Planning and Impact
on Future Generations

Building a thriving business isn't just about achieving short-term success—it's about creating a legacy that endures. Legacy planning ensures that the values, vision, and impact of a business or leader continue to influence future generations. This section explores how companies and leaders align their day-to-day actions with long-term goals, fostering a lasting imprint on their industries, communities, and stakeholders.

At the heart of legacy-building is purpose-driven leadership. Leaders highlighted in these case studies focus not only on profits but also on how their decisions affect society and the broader business landscape. Their work extends beyond quarterly results, incorporating sustainable practices, ethical policies, and community engagement to leave a positive impact that resonates far into the future. These leaders show that a well-planned legacy reflects a commitment to societal betterment and long-term value creation.

A key part of legacy creation is succession planning—ensuring the smooth transition of leadership to sustain the organization's vision and momentum. The case studies emphasize that successful businesses develop systems to train future leaders who embody the organization's core values. By cultivating talent within the organization and mentoring the next generation of leaders, these businesses remain resilient across transitions and maintain their innovative edge.

Another component of legacy-building is philanthropy and community involvement. The companies featured demonstrate that social impact initiatives—such as giving back to communities, supporting education, or engaging in environmental sustainability—enhance their reputation and build goodwill. These actions align with consumers' growing interest in supporting brands that are socially responsible and committed to positive change.

Incorporating long-term thinking into strategic planning ensures that a company's legacy evolves naturally alongside its growth. Leaders adopt flexible frameworks that allow the organization to adapt and expand while staying rooted in core principles. Whether it's expanding into new markets, entering partnerships with like-minded organizations, or innovating for future challenges, these leaders think beyond immediate returns, focusing on sustainable progress.

Ultimately, strategic legacy planning is about building something greater than yourself. The impact of a business becomes more meaningful and memorable when it reflects values that inspire future generations to carry forward its mission. These case studies illustrate how leaders and organizations align vision, values, and action to create a legacy that stands the test of time, proving that true success lies not just in what you build today, but in what you leave behind.

Learning by Reflection and Experimentation

In an ever-changing business landscape, success isn't just about having the right answers—it's about continuous learning through reflection and experimentation. The companies and leaders highlighted in this section demonstrate that progress comes from actively engaging with experiences, reflecting on outcomes, and iterating to improve. Learning is not a passive process but an ongoing cycle of trying, assessing, and refining approaches to meet evolving needs and challenges.

Reflection plays a crucial role in identifying what works and what doesn't. Leaders and teams take time to analyze results, review decisions, and consider the lessons learned from both successes and failures. The case studies show how businesses establish feedback loops and post-mortem reviews, ensuring that every action—whether a campaign, launch, or strategy—yields insights for future improvements. Self-awareness, transparency, and accountability are emphasized as essential elements of reflection, creating a culture where growth is driven by continuous self-assessment.

Alongside reflection, experimentation becomes a powerful driver of innovation and adaptability. Businesses that embrace experimentation are not afraid to take calculated risks. They pilot new initiatives, test products in small markets, or run experimental marketing campaigns to gather data before making larger investments. Agile methodologies, split testing, and iterative design approaches help these companies learn quickly, pivot efficiently, and optimize strategies based on real-time feedback.

Failure is treated as an integral part of learning rather than a setback. Leaders foster an environment where mistakes are viewed as opportunities for growth, encouraging employees to experiment without fear of punishment. This "fail fast, learn faster" mindset ensures businesses remain innovative and adaptive. Many case studies highlight organizations that turned failures into breakthroughs by refining their ideas after initial setbacks, ultimately achieving greater success than anticipated.

In this section, readers will discover how to apply reflective and experimental practices to their own businesses. It emphasizes the importance of documenting lessons, engaging with feedback, and fostering a culture of learning. Businesses that thrive in the long term are those that treat reflection and experimentation as ongoing processes, using each experience as a stepping stone toward improvement.

By integrating reflective practices and embracing experimentation as a tool for growth, leaders ensure their organizations stay flexible, innovative, and prepared for future challenges. This section serves as a reminder that learning is never complete—the most successful businesses are those that remain curious, iterative, and open to change.

How to Use this Volume

This volume, "74 Case Studies in Growth, Digital Presence, and Legacy Building," is designed to be both practical and flexible, serving as a valuable resource whether you are a business owner, leader, entrepreneur, marketer, or professional looking to grow personally and professionally. Here's how you can get the most out of this book:

1. Read Sequentially or Select by Need

Each chapter is organized around a specific topic—such as building a standout brand, time management, digital marketing, or social media strategies. You can read the book from cover to cover to develop a well-rounded understanding, or jump directly to the sections most relevant to your current needs or challenges. Whether you're looking to optimize a workflow, develop a brand, or engage a digital audience, the case studies are designed to stand alone or integrate cohesively.

2. Apply Lessons Through Reflection and Action

The key to benefiting from these case studies lies in applying what you learn. At the end of each section, take time to reflect on how the insights align with your goals. Use the examples to guide your next steps—whether it's refining your business strategy, developing a new product, or launching a digital campaign. Keep notes on which lessons resonate most and how they could translate into actionable plans for your business.

3. Use as a Discussion Tool for Teams

This volume is ideal for team discussions and collaborative learning. Managers and team leaders can use specific case studies as conversation starters to explore new ideas and problem-solving approaches. Try applying the lessons to current projects or challenges your team faces. Encourage team members to share how they interpret the case studies, fostering collaboration and shared learning.

4. Integrate Insights into Your Digital Strategy

Given the focus on digital presence and brand building, this book offers actionable advice for enhancing your online visibility, building communities, and engaging with audiences. Use the sections on social media, storytelling, and SEO strategies to refine your digital efforts. Each chapter contains practical frameworks and tools you can implement directly into your business or marketing strategies.

5. Reflect on Legacy and Long-Term Impact

Throughout the volume, you will find case studies focusing on legacy-building strategies. Use these insights to align your day-to-day operations with long-term goals. Think beyond immediate profits—ask yourself how your work today contributes to a lasting impact. Consider how the lessons in this book can shape both your personal leadership journey and the future direction of your business.

6. Revisit the Book as Your Business Evolves

As your goals and circumstances change, the challenges you face will evolve. This volume is designed to be a long-term companion—a resource you can return to whenever you encounter new challenges or opportunities. Whether you're scaling operations, entering new markets, or reimagining your brand, you'll find timeless insights within these pages to guide your path forward.

This book is not just a collection of case studies—it's a tool for personal and professional growth, offering insight, inspiration, and practical strategies for building a thriving business with long-lasting impact. Use it actively, reflect deeply, and apply the lessons boldly—your path to success starts here.

Conclusion

"74 Case Studies in Growth, Digital Presence, and Legacy Building" offers a comprehensive guide to building thriving enterprises through thoughtful planning, continuous innovation, and strategic digital engagement. The case studies demonstrate that long-term success requires both vision and execution, balancing sustainable growth with a focus on future impact.

Whether you are an entrepreneur, executive, or professional, this volume provides real-world insights and actionable strategies to help you navigate challenges, embrace digital transformation, and leave a lasting legacy. With each story, you'll gain tools to turn ideas into reality, build strong brands, and shape your own path to enduring success.

As you engage with the lessons shared in this book, remember that growth is an ongoing process. It requires reflection, adaptability, and persistence. The tools, insights, and frameworks presented here are meant to serve as companions on your journey, offering guidance for both present challenges and future ambitions. By applying the lessons from these case studies, you can build not just a business, but a legacy that stands the test of time.

This is your invitation to grow boldly, lead authentically, and make a meaningful impact—one decision, strategy, and story at a time.

CHAPTER ONE

Shaping an Unstoppable Vision

At the core of every thriving business lies a vision that goes far beyond spreadsheets and financial forecasts. Vision forms the foundation of purpose—it reflects what drives you as a leader and why your business exists beyond making a profit. A compelling vision doesn't just steer internal decisions; it resonates with employees, customers, investors, and partners, aligning every effort toward a common goal. It provides clarity in times of uncertainty and motivates your team to push forward, even when challenges seem overwhelming. Crafting a vision that inspires is the first essential step in transforming an idea into an enduring enterprise.

The process begins with understanding your "why." Aristotle believed that purpose and meaning define human flourishing, and businesses are no different— vision must connect with something greater than short-term goals. Modern leaders, such as David Droga, the mastermind behind creative storytelling in advertising, know the power of crafting a narrative that taps into emotions.

Similarly, Stephen King, with his unparalleled talent for weaving complex stories, shows how a clear vision can shape not only individual projects but also a lifelong legacy. A business's vision should express not just what it does but why it matters. This deeper purpose sparks passion in teams and cultivates long-term loyalty among customers. In today's competitive landscape, where consumers align with brands that share their values, a meaningful vision becomes a point of differentiation.

Turning a powerful vision into reality requires more than imagination—it requires strategic focus and execution. Margaret Thatcher, known for her unwavering resolve, demonstrated that vision without action is mere rhetoric. Every decision, no matter how small, must align with the larger purpose. Similarly, Angela Clarke—with her expertise in building resilient organizations—shows how vision can be woven into every aspect of operations, from product development to employee engagement. When vision forms the foundation of a business, it becomes a strategic compass, guiding choices and shaping brand identity. Leaders who consistently align actions with their vision—like Alex Mercer, who rebuilt his business after setbacks—illustrate how every step forward, no matter how difficult, can bring the vision closer to reality.

However, vision must be adaptable to thrive. The business landscape evolves rapidly, and visionary leaders know that remaining rigid can lead to failure. Both Celeste Harper, with her creative agility in adapting to shifting markets, and Thatcher, with her pragmatic approach to unforeseen challenges, exemplify the importance of balancing focus with flexibility. Visionary leadership is not about unwavering stubbornness but about staying true to a mission while pivoting strategically when needed.

This chapter will offer practical insights into crafting and refining your business vision. Drawing from the journeys of leaders like Droga, King, and Harper, you'll explore how to discover and articulate the core purpose of your business. You'll learn techniques for developing a vision that resonates both internally and externally—one that motivates teams and attracts loyal customers. Vision becomes powerful when it guides decision-making and shapes your organization's story and culture.

By the end of this chapter, you'll have the tools to craft a vision that not only inspires action but also fosters resilience. Whether through storytelling, branding, or leadership, you'll explore how to communicate your vision effectively to stakeholders, just as these case study leaders did. A well-defined vision becomes the foundation of your strategy, the backbone of your brand, and the reason customers, employees, and partners will align with you. When your vision inspires action and evolution, it lays the groundwork for building something far greater than a business—it becomes the blueprint for an empire.

―――――――――

Aristotle's Success Story: The Philosopher Who Shaped Western Thought

"We are what we repeatedly do. Excellence, then, is not an act, but a habit."
— ARISTOTLE, PHILOSOPHER

Aristotle, one of the most influential figures in human history, was a Greek philosopher whose work laid the foundation for many disciplines, including philosophy, science, ethics, and politics. Born in 384 BCE in the city of Stagira in northern Greece, Aristotle's teachings and writings have profoundly influenced Western thought for over two millennia. His journey from a student at Plato's Academy to becoming the tutor of Alexander the Great and the founder of his own philosophical school reflects a life dedicated to the pursuit of knowledge and wisdom.

Early Life: A Love for Learning
Aristotle was born into a family closely connected to the Macedonian court. His father, Nicomachus, served as the personal physician to King Amyntas of Macedon. This early exposure to both science and politics likely shaped Aristotle's interest in biology and governance. After his father's death, Aristotle was sent to Athens at the age of 17 to study at Plato's Academy, the most prestigious educational institution in Greece at the time.

3

Student of Plato: Shaping His Philosophical Foundations

Aristotle spent 20 years at Plato's Academy, where he immersed himself in philosophical debates and developed his early ideas. Although he greatly admired Plato, Aristotle's views diverged from his teacher's. While Plato emphasized abstract ideals and forms, Aristotle was more interested in empirical observation—seeking knowledge from the natural world and practical experience rather than purely theoretical concepts.

This difference in philosophy eventually led Aristotle to establish his own school, with a focus on critical thinking, ethics, and scientific inquiry. His willingness to challenge established ideas would define his legacy as a thinker.

The Macedonian Court and Tutoring Alexander the Great

After Plato's death in 347 BCE, Aristotle left Athens and traveled to Macedon, where he was invited by King Philip II to tutor his son, Alexander—the future Alexander the Great. Aristotle's role as Alexander's tutor gave him access to political power and influence.

During this time, Aristotle likely introduced Alexander to concepts of governance, ethics, and leadership, shaping the young prince's worldview. Aristotle's teachings emphasized the importance of reason, justice, and virtue in leadership, values that influenced Alexander throughout his conquests.

Founding the Lyceum: Aristotle's Own School of Thought

In 335 BCE, Aristotle returned to Athens and founded his own school, the Lyceum. Unlike Plato's Academy, the Lyceum emphasized practical learning through empirical observation and research. Aristotle and his students, known as Peripatetics, engaged in discussions while walking around the school's covered walkways. The Lyceum became a center for inquiry into a wide range of subjects, including biology, physics, logic, ethics, politics, and rhetoric.

Aristotle's work at the Lyceum was groundbreaking. He collected and classified plants and animals, laying the foundation for natural sciences. His method of logical reasoning, known as syllogism, remains a fundamental aspect of modern logic. Aristotle's writings explored human nature, ethics, the role of government, and the purpose of life, providing the framework for later developments in Western philosophy.

Philosophical Contributions: A Legacy of Knowledge

Aristotle's writings cover an extraordinary range of subjects. Some of his most significant works include:

- **Metaphysics**: Examines the nature of reality, exploring concepts like being, substance, and cause.

- **Nicomachean Ethics**: Discusses the nature of virtue, happiness, and the moral life. Aristotle believed that the highest good is eudaimonia—a state of human flourishing achieved through virtuous living.

- **Politics**: Explores the role of government and the relationship between individuals and the state, emphasizing the importance of civic participation and justice.

- **Poetics**: Analyzes literature and drama, offering insights into tragedy and storytelling that remain influential in literary theory.

- **On the Soul (De Anima)**: Investigates the nature of the human soul and the relationship between the body and mind.

Aristotle's scientific approach to knowledge, focusing on observation and classification, also laid the foundation for fields like biology, zoology, and physics. Although some of his scientific ideas were later disproved, his methodology influenced the development of the scientific method centuries later.

Challenges and Final Years

After the death of Alexander the Great in 323 BCE, anti-Macedonian sentiment in Athens grew. Because of his ties to the Macedonian court, Aristotle was charged with impiety, similar to the fate of Socrates. Rather than face trial, Aristotle fled Athens, famously saying, "I will not allow the Athenians to sin twice against philosophy."

Aristotle retired to Chalcis, on the island of Euboea, where he spent the remaining years of his life. He passed away in 322 BCE, at the age of 62, leaving behind an intellectual legacy that would shape Western thought for centuries.

Legacy: The Father of Western Philosophy

Aristotle's influence on philosophy, science, and ethics is unparalleled. His ideas remained central to Western thought for centuries, shaping the intellectual framework of the Middle Ages through the works of scholars like Thomas Aquinas. During the Renaissance, his writings were rediscovered and integrated into scientific and philosophical discussions, laying the groundwork for modern disciplines.

Even today, Aristotle's concepts of virtue ethics, logic, and scientific inquiry continue to influence fields ranging from philosophy and biology to political science and literature. His ability to synthesize knowledge across multiple domains has earned him a place as one of the greatest thinkers in human history.

Conclusion: A Life Dedicated to Knowledge and Inquiry

Aristotle's journey from a student in Plato's Academy to the founder of the Lyceum reflects a life dedicated to the pursuit of knowledge. His belief in empirical observation and rational thought revolutionized how humans understand the world, influencing countless generations of scholars and thinkers. Aristotle's legacy is a testament to the enduring power of curiosity, logic, and inquiry in shaping human progress. His works remind us that knowledge is not merely an accumulation of facts but a tool for understanding the world and living a virtuous life.

David Droga's Success Story: Revolutionizing Advertising with Creativity and Purpose

"In a digital world, print media is not just nostalgia; it's a tangible expression of your brand that cuts through the noise with the quiet power of touch."
— DAVID DROGA, FOUNDER OF DROGA5

David Droga is one of the most influential figures in modern advertising, known for redefining how brands connect with audiences through creativity, innovation, and storytelling. As the founder of Droga5, a globally acclaimed advertising agency, and now the CEO of Accenture Song, Droga has built a career marked by bold campaigns that challenge conventional thinking. His journey from a young creative talent in Australia to a global advertising icon reflects a relentless pursuit of excellence and a belief in the power of ideas to shape culture.

Early Life: A Passion for Creativity

David Droga was born in 1968 in Perth, Australia, and grew up as the youngest of five children in a family that nurtured curiosity and creativity. From a young age, Droga demonstrated a natural flair for storytelling and creative thinking. He spent his childhood exploring various creative outlets, which would later inspire his career in advertising.

Droga attended The King's School in Sydney, where he discovered a passion for the arts. After high school, he pursued studies in communications and advertising, determined to make a mark in the creative industry. His ambition to push boundaries was evident even in his early years, setting the stage for his rise in advertising.

Early Career: Climbing the Advertising Ranks

Droga began his career in Australia, working for leading agencies like Ogilvy and Saatchi & Saatchi. His talent for crafting innovative campaigns quickly set him apart, and at the age of 22, Droga became the youngest-ever Creative Director of OMON, an Australian agency. This early success earned him industry recognition and a reputation as one of the most promising young talents in advertising.

Eager to make an impact on a global stage, Droga moved to Singapore to become Executive Creative Director of Saatchi & Saatchi Asia. Under his leadership, the agency thrived, producing award-winning campaigns that gained international acclaim. At just 29 years old, Droga was promoted to Worldwide Creative Director of Saatchi & Saatchi, based in London. This role cemented his position as one of the top creative minds in the industry.

Founding Droga5: Building an Iconic Agency

In 2006, Droga took a bold step by founding Droga5 in New York City, with the ambition of creating an agency that would prioritize ideas, creativity, and impact over traditional marketing approaches. The name "Droga5" was inspired by a label his mother used to sew onto his clothes as the fifth child in the family.

From the beginning, Droga5's mission was to challenge the status quo of advertising. The agency quickly made a name for itself with innovative, culturally relevant campaigns. One of Droga5's early successes was the "Great Schlep" campaign for Barack Obama's 2008 presidential campaign, encouraging young

Jewish voters to convince their grandparents in Florida to vote for Obama. The campaign demonstrated the power of creative storytelling to influence social change.

Award-Winning Campaigns and Global Recognition

Droga5 became known for creating memorable and meaningful work for clients like Under Armour, The New York Times, Google, and HBO. The agency's "Rule Yourself" campaign for Under Armour, featuring Michael Phelps, and "The Truth Is Hard" campaign for The New York Times, were widely celebrated for their emotional resonance and cultural relevance. These campaigns reflected Droga's belief that advertising should not just sell products but also tell compelling stories and foster connections.

Under Droga's leadership, the agency received numerous accolades, including Agency of the Year honors multiple times from publications like Adweek and Advertising Age. Droga himself became the most awarded creative of all time, earning more than 70 Cannes Lions, including multiple Grand Prix awards.

Joining Accenture Song: Merging Creativity and Technology

In 2019, Droga5 was acquired by Accenture Interactive (now known as Accenture Song), a move that reflected the evolving landscape of marketing, where creativity and technology intersect. In 2021, David Droga was named CEO and Creative Chairman of Accenture Song, taking on the challenge of integrating creative excellence with data-driven technology.

In this new role, Droga aims to redefine the future of advertising by combining the storytelling expertise of Droga5 with Accenture's technological capabilities. His vision is to create work that is both innovative and impactful, helping brands stay relevant in an increasingly complex digital world.

Leadership Philosophy: Creativity with Purpose

David Droga's success can be attributed not only to his creative talent but also to his leadership philosophy. He believes that the best advertising is both meaningful and culturally relevant, connecting brands with consumers on an emotional level. Droga encourages his teams to push boundaries, take risks, and embrace failure as part of the creative process.

His focus on purpose-driven work has also shaped Droga5's identity. Many of the agency's most successful campaigns address social issues, demonstrating that brands can have a positive impact beyond profit. This belief in the power of storytelling to drive change has earned Droga respect not only as a creative leader but also as an industry visionary.

Legacy and Impact

David Droga's influence on the advertising industry is profound. He has redefined what it means to create great work, blending creativity with cultural relevance and proving that advertising can be a force for good. His success with Droga5, now under the umbrella of Accenture Song, demonstrates his ability to adapt and innovate in a rapidly changing industry.

Droga's legacy lies not only in the awards he has won but also in the impact his work has had on culture and society. From political campaigns to empowering brands, Droga has shown that creativity can inspire action and shape conversations. His journey from a young creative in Australia to one of the most influential figures in global advertising reflects a passion for ideas, a commitment to excellence, and a belief in the transformative power of storytelling.

Conclusion: A Visionary at the Forefront of Advertising

David Droga's story is one of bold ambition, relentless creativity, and thoughtful leadership. His ability to challenge the status quo and create work that resonates with audiences has made him a trailblazer in advertising. As he continues to lead Accenture Song into the future, Droga's vision for combining creativity with technology promises to shape the next era of marketing. His journey is a testament to the power of risk-taking, innovation, and purpose-driven storytelling, inspiring future generations of creatives and business leaders alike.

Margaret Thatcher's Success Story: The Iron Lady Who Transformed Britain

"Plan your work for today and every day, then work your plan."
— MARGARET THATCHER, FORMER PRIME MINISTER
OF THE UNITED KINGDOM

Margaret Thatcher, Britain's first female Prime Minister, was a trailblazing political leader whose transformative policies reshaped the United Kingdom's economy and politics. Known as the "Iron Lady" for her uncompromising style, Thatcher's leadership was marked by her commitment to free markets, individual responsibility, and reduced government intervention. Her journey from a modest upbringing to becoming one of the most influential leaders of the 20th century is a testament to her determination, ambition, and belief in the power of conviction.

Early Life: A Modest Upbringing in Grantham
Margaret Hilda Roberts was born on October 13, 1925, in Grantham, England, to Alfred and Beatrice Roberts. Her father, a grocer and local politician, instilled in her values of self-reliance, hard work, and thrift, which would later shape her political philosophy. Growing up above the family grocery store, Thatcher learned the importance of discipline and responsibility from an early age.

A talented student, Thatcher attended Oxford University, where she studied chemistry at Somerville College. After graduating, she worked briefly as a research chemist but soon found herself drawn to politics, inspired by her father's involvement in local government and her interest in current affairs.

Early Political Career: Breaking into Parliament
Thatcher's political career began in earnest in the 1950s, when she joined the Conservative Party. In 1959, she was elected Member of Parliament (MP) for Finchley, representing the constituency for more than three decades. Early in her career, Thatcher focused on social issues, including education and housing, and quickly gained a reputation for her hard work and sharp intelligence.

In 1970, she was appointed Secretary of State for Education and Science under Prime Minister Edward Heath. During her tenure, she faced backlash for cutting subsidies for free milk in schools, a decision that earned her the nickname

"Thatcher, the Milk Snatcher." Despite the controversy, she remained undeterred, committed to making difficult choices in the face of public criticism.

The Road to Leadership: Becoming Party Leader

Thatcher's ascent to the top of British politics began in 1975, when she successfully challenged Edward Heath for the leadership of the Conservative Party. Her victory marked a significant milestone, as she became the first woman to lead a major political party in the United Kingdom. At the time, Britain was grappling with economic challenges, including high inflation, labor strikes, and growing public dissatisfaction with government policies.

Thatcher's message of economic reform, smaller government, and individual responsibility resonated with voters, and she led the Conservative Party to victory in the 1979 general election, becoming the first female Prime Minister in British history.

Prime Minister: Reshaping Britain's Economy and Society

Thatcher's tenure as Prime Minister, from 1979 to 1990, was defined by her commitment to free-market principles and a radical restructuring of the British economy. She sought to reduce the power of trade unions, cut government spending, and promote privatization of state-owned industries. Her government introduced reforms that curbed inflation, deregulated industries, and encouraged entrepreneurship, ushering in an era of economic liberalization.

One of Thatcher's defining moments came during the miners' strike of 1984–1985, when she stood firm against the striking coal miners, determined to reduce the influence of labor unions. The strike ended in defeat for the miners and marked a turning point in Britain's industrial landscape, with many industries shifting toward privatization.

The Falklands War: A Test of Leadership

In 1982, Thatcher faced a significant challenge when Argentina invaded the Falkland Islands, a British overseas territory. Thatcher responded decisively by sending a military task force to reclaim the islands. The swift victory in the Falklands War boosted her popularity and solidified her reputation as a strong and determined leader on the global stage.

International Influence: The Iron Lady on the World Stage
Thatcher's leadership extended beyond domestic reforms. She developed close relationships with other world leaders, including U.S. President Ronald Reagan, with whom she shared a mutual commitment to free-market economics and opposition to Soviet communism. Together, they championed the principles of economic liberalism and Western democracy, becoming key allies during the Cold War.

Her tough stance against the Soviet Union earned her the nickname "Iron Lady" from a Soviet journalist, a title she embraced as a symbol of her strength and resolve.

Challenges and Resignation
Despite her successes, Thatcher's leadership was not without controversy. Her Poll Tax policy, introduced in 1990, sparked widespread protests and public opposition, becoming a major source of political unrest. Members of her own party began to question her leadership, and she faced mounting pressure to step down.

In November 1990, Thatcher resigned as Prime Minister after losing the support of her Cabinet and party. Although her departure marked the end of her time in office, her influence on British politics and the Conservative Party remained strong.

Later Life and Legacy
After leaving office, Thatcher remained active in public life, delivering speeches and writing memoirs, including "The Downing Street Years." She continued to advocate for conservative principles and remained a respected figure in global politics. In 1992, she was made a Baroness, taking her seat in the House of Lords as Baroness Thatcher of Kesteven.

Thatcher's health began to decline in her later years, and she passed away on April 8, 2013, at the age of 87. Her death marked the end of an era, but her legacy as a transformative leader endures.

Impact and Legacy: The Iron Lady's Influence
Margaret Thatcher's impact on Britain and the world is profound. Her policies of privatization, deregulation, and individual responsibility reshaped the British

economy and influenced governments worldwide. While critics argue that her policies increased inequality and weakened social safety nets, supporters credit her with reviving the British economy and restoring national pride.

Thatcher's legacy extends beyond her policies—she broke barriers as the first woman to lead Britain and inspired future generations of female leaders. Her belief in self-reliance, courage, and conviction continues to resonate with political leaders and thinkers across the globe.

Conclusion: A Trailblazing Legacy of Leadership
Margaret Thatcher's journey from a grocer's daughter to the first female Prime Minister of the United Kingdom exemplifies the power of determination, ambition, and belief in one's convictions. Her tenure as Prime Minister was marked by bold reforms, international leadership, and unwavering resolve. Whether admired or criticized, Thatcher's influence on politics, economics, and leadership is undeniable, cementing her place in history as the Iron Lady who transformed Britain and inspired the world.

Stephen King's Success Story: Master of Horror and Storytelling

"Understanding the grant of rights clause isn't just paperwork—it's the blueprint to how your book lives in the world. Handle it wisely, and you dictate the terms of your work's journey." — STEPHEN KING, AUTHOR

Stephen King, one of the most prolific and successful authors of all time, has captivated readers with his ability to blend horror, suspense, and the supernatural with deeply human experiences. From a struggling writer living in a trailer to a global literary icon, King's journey reflects his resilience, imagination, and love for storytelling. With over 60 novels, 200 short stories, and numerous film and television adaptations, King's influence on literature and pop culture is unparalleled.

Early Life: A Love for Books and Imagination

Stephen Edwin King was born on September 21, 1947, in Portland, Maine. Raised primarily by his mother after his father abandoned the family, King had a modest upbringing that shaped much of his writing. From a young age, he found comfort and inspiration in books, especially horror and science fiction stories. King devoured comic books and novels by authors like H.P. Lovecraft and Richard Matheson, whose influence would later be reflected in his work.

As a teenager, King began writing stories of his own, submitting them to magazines. Though many of his early attempts were rejected, he never gave up on his dream of becoming a writer. His persistence during these formative years would prove essential to his later success.

Education and Early Struggles: Writing Against the Odds

King attended the University of Maine, where he majored in English and contributed stories to the campus newspaper. During this time, he met Tabitha Spruce, who would become both his wife and an essential source of support throughout his career. After graduating in 1970, King struggled to find steady work. He took various odd jobs, including teaching high school English, while continuing to write stories in his free time.

The early years of King's marriage were marked by financial difficulties. The couple lived in a small trailer, and King wrote short stories for men's magazines to make ends meet. Despite the challenges, he kept working on his first novel in the evenings, driven by the hope that his efforts would eventually pay off.

Breakthrough with *Carrie*

King's big break came in 1974 with the publication of his first novel, Carrie. The story, which follows a bullied teenage girl with telekinetic powers, almost never saw the light of day. Frustrated with his initial draft, King famously threw the manuscript into the trash. Fortunately, Tabitha retrieved it, encouraged him to finish it, and provided invaluable feedback.

When *Carrie* was published, it became an instant success, selling over one million copies in its first year. The book's popularity, along with a successful film adaptation, launched King into the spotlight and gave him the financial freedom to pursue writing full-time.

Building a Literary Empire: Iconic Novels and Adaptations

Following the success of *Carrie*, King published a series of novels that cemented his reputation as the master of horror. His next works, including 'Salem's Lot (1975), The Shining (1977), and The Stand (1978), showcased his ability to weave intricate plots with compelling characters. King's writing tapped into readers' deepest fears—whether through haunted hotels, vampires, or apocalyptic plagues.

In addition to his novels, King also wrote short stories and novellas, many of which have been adapted into films, such as "The Shawshank Redemption," "Stand by Me," and "The Green Mile." His stories go beyond horror, often exploring themes of friendship, redemption, and the resilience of the human spirit.

Battling Personal Demons: Addiction and Recovery

Despite his success, King struggled with alcoholism and drug addiction throughout much of the 1980s. At one point, he feared that his substance abuse would derail his career and personal life. In 1987, after an intervention led by Tabitha and their children, King committed to getting sober. His battle with addiction deeply influenced his later works, including Doctor Sleep (2013), a sequel to *The Shining* that deals with recovery and redemption.

King's ability to confront his personal demons and channel them into his writing added emotional depth to his work, endearing him to readers who found his characters relatable and authentic.

Reinvention and Critical Acclaim

King continued to evolve as a writer, experimenting with genres beyond horror. In 1982, he published The Dark Tower: The Gunslinger, the first in a series of eight novels blending fantasy, horror, and Western elements. *The Dark Tower* series became one of his most ambitious projects, earning a devoted following and solidifying King's place as a versatile storyteller.

Throughout the 1990s and 2000s, King released several critically acclaimed novels, including Misery, It, The Green Mile, and 11/22/63, showcasing his ability to tell stories that transcend genres. Many of these works were adapted into successful films and miniseries, further expanding his influence.

Near-Death Experience and Creative Renaissance

In 1999, King was struck by a van while walking near his home in Maine, leaving him with life-threatening injuries. The accident forced him to confront his mortality and temporarily halted his writing. However, King's recovery marked the beginning of a creative renaissance. His determination to keep writing despite his injuries underscored his deep passion for storytelling.

In the years following the accident, King published several more bestsellers, including Under the Dome and Revival, proving that his ability to captivate readers had not diminished. He also began collaborating with his son, Joe Hill, and published works with Tabitha, highlighting his family's creative spirit.

Stephen King's Legacy: Master of Horror and Beyond

Over the course of his career, Stephen King has published more than 60 novels, 200 short stories, and numerous non-fiction works. His books have sold over 350 million copies, making him one of the most commercially successful authors in history. His influence extends beyond literature into film, television, and popular culture, with countless adaptations of his work becoming iconic in their own right.

King's storytelling resonates with readers not just because of the scares, but because of his deep understanding of human nature. His characters, often flawed and vulnerable, confront fears that are both supernatural and profoundly personal.

Philosophy and Writing Approach

King's writing philosophy, outlined in his memoir "On Writing: A Memoir of the Craft," emphasizes the importance of discipline and persistence. He famously advises aspiring writers to "read a lot and write a lot." His straightforward, conversational style has made him a relatable figure in the literary world, inspiring countless writers to pursue their dreams.

King's work ethic is legendary—he writes every day, even on holidays, maintaining a goal of producing at least 2,000 words per day. This relentless dedication to his craft is a key factor behind his extraordinary success.

Conclusion: A Literary Icon with Enduring Influence

Stephen King's journey from a struggling writer living in a trailer to an internationally renowned author reflects the power of imagination, persistence, and resilience. His ability to tell stories that explore fear, hope, and redemption has touched the lives of millions of readers. King's influence on literature, film, and pop culture is unparalleled, and his work continues to captivate new generations.

Whether scaring readers with tales of haunted hotels or inspiring them with stories of friendship and survival, King remains a master storyteller. His legacy as the "King of Horror" will endure, reminding us that great stories have the power to thrill, heal, and connect us across time and space.

Celeste Harper's Success Story: Mastering the Art of Words and Captivating Audiences

"Crafting a book blurb is like brewing a powerful potion; it should entice with its aroma, promise with its taste, and deliver with its effects, compelling readers to sip—and then gulp down the whole story."
— CELESTE HARPER, COPYWRITING MAESTRO

Celeste Harper, known as a copywriting maestro, has built a remarkable career through her ability to craft compelling narratives and captivating book blurbs. Her skill in transforming ideas into engaging prose has made her one of the most sought-after talents in the literary and marketing world. Harper's journey to success is defined by a deep passion for language, a keen understanding of storytelling, and an ability to connect with audiences through the power of words.

Early Life: A Love for Storytelling
Celeste Harper's fascination with language began at an early age. Growing up with a passion for books, she spent her childhood immersed in stories, developing a knack for identifying what made them compelling. Harper's early experiences with reading nurtured her love for storytelling, planting the seeds for a future in writing and creative communication.

Her academic background in literature and communications provided a solid foundation for her career. During her college years, Harper discovered the art of copywriting, where she saw the potential to blend her storytelling skills with marketing principles. This realization inspired her to pursue a career that combined creativity with strategy.

Finding Her Niche: The Art of the Book Blurb

Harper found her niche in the world of publishing, where she quickly developed a reputation for writing exceptional book blurbs. Her signature style—concise, enticing, and packed with intrigue—soon became the gold standard. Harper's philosophy is best captured in her now-famous quote: *"Crafting a book blurb is like brewing a powerful potion; it should entice with its aroma, promise with its taste, and deliver with its effects, compelling readers to sip—and then gulp down the whole story."*

Her ability to capture the essence of a story in just a few sentences turned book blurbs from mere summaries into irresistible invitations for readers. Publishers and authors alike sought her expertise, recognizing the impact of a well-crafted blurb on book sales.

Building a Brand: From Freelancer to Copywriting Icon

Harper's talent and dedication allowed her to quickly transition from freelance gigs to building a personal brand as a copywriting expert. She expanded her services beyond book blurbs to marketing campaigns, product descriptions, and branding strategies, helping clients across industries communicate their stories effectively.

What set Harper apart was her empathy-driven approach—she didn't just write to sell; she wrote to connect. Whether working with best-selling authors or small independent publishers, Harper took the time to understand the heart of each project, crafting words that resonated with target audiences.

Workshops and Mentorship: Sharing the Craft

As Harper's reputation grew, she began hosting workshops and mentoring aspiring copywriters. Her workshops focused on the intricacies of short-form storytelling, emphasizing that even a few words could evoke powerful emotions. Harper became known not just as a skilled writer but as a generous mentor, inspiring a new generation of writers to pursue careers in creative communication.

Her insights on branding, audience engagement, and persuasive writing became invaluable resources for those looking to excel in copywriting. Harper's ability to demystify the creative process earned her a loyal following among aspiring writers and seasoned professionals alike.

Challenges and Growth: Adapting to the Digital Age

Like any successful professional, Harper faced challenges as the publishing landscape evolved. The shift from traditional print to digital platforms required new strategies for engaging readers. Harper embraced these changes, using her versatility to adapt her writing for social media campaigns, website content, and e-commerce platforms.

Her adaptability and willingness to embrace new technologies kept her at the forefront of the copywriting industry. Harper's work now extends to writing ad copy, newsletters, and brand messaging for a wide range of industries, demonstrating her ability to evolve with changing market demands.

Legacy and Influence: A Copywriting Maestro

Today, Celeste Harper is recognized as a leading voice in the world of copywriting. Her work continues to influence how authors, publishers, and brands communicate with their audiences. Harper's ability to blend creativity with strategy has set new standards in the industry, inspiring countless professionals to approach writing as both an art and a science.

Her belief in the power of words to create connections has left a lasting impact. Through her workshops, mentorship, and published works, Harper continues to share her expertise, ensuring that her legacy as a copywriting maestro endures.

Conclusion: A Master of Storytelling and Connection

Celeste Harper's journey to success exemplifies the power of passion, creativity, and adaptability. From her early love for storytelling to becoming one of the most sought-after copywriters, Harper's career reflects a commitment to excellence and an understanding of how words can inspire action.

Her ability to capture the essence of a story in just a few lines has made her an indispensable figure in publishing and marketing. Whether crafting book blurbs or brand narratives, Harper's influence extends far beyond the words she writes—her work embodies the power of language to engage, connect, and inspire.

Angela Clarke's Success Story: From Fashionista to Bestselling Crime Author

"Optimizing your Amazon presence is like setting the stage for a grand performance where every element of your book's page plays a part in captivating the audience and commanding the spotlight."
— ANGELA CLARKE, DIGITAL MARKETING EXPERT

"Release day is your grand gala, where every tweet, post, and event must sing in harmony, transforming your book launch into an unforgettable symphony of success." — ANGELA CLARKE, MARKETING EXPERT

Angela Clarke is a British author, playwright, screenwriter, and broadcaster, best known for her Social Media Murders series. Her journey from fashion columnist to acclaimed crime writer showcases her versatility, creativity, and determination. Clarke's career is built on storytelling that explores the impact of modern life and technology—particularly the dark side of social media.

Early Life and Career: The Fashion World Beckons
Before breaking into fiction, Clarke's creative career began in the fashion industry, where she worked as a columnist. She gained attention through her anonymous column, "Confessions of a Fashionista," for the *Daily Mail*. The column, which offered humorous insights into the fashion world, resonated with readers. Clarke later revealed her identity and compiled her experiences into a memoir, *Confessions of a Fashionista* (2013). The book was praised for its wit and relatability, offering a behind-the-scenes look at the glamorous but often absurd realities of the industry.

The Shift to Crime Fiction: A New Chapter Begins
Clarke's transition from fashion to fiction was marked by the publication of her debut crime novel, Follow Me (2016). This fast-paced thriller explores the dangers of social media, following the investigation of the "Hashtag Murderer," who taunts the public by posting clues about his next victim online. *Follow Me* was an instant success, becoming Amazon's Rising Star Debut of the Month and earning nominations for the Crime Writers' Association Dagger in the Library and the Dead Good Reader Page Turner Award.

The success of *Follow Me* led to the development of the Social Media Murders series, which includes Watch Me and Trust Me. Clarke's thrillers are known for their engaging plots, dark humor, and exploration of contemporary issues like online privacy, influence, and obsession.

Screenwriting, Playwriting, and Beyond

Angela Clarke's talents extend beyond the world of fiction. In addition to her novels, she is a playwright and screenwriter, bringing her storytelling skills to stage and screen. Her work as a broadcaster has also allowed her to share her expertise on books, creativity, and social issues. Clarke's ability to balance multiple creative fields reflects her commitment to storytelling in all its forms. She is also a Fellow of the Royal Society of Arts, highlighting her contributions to the arts and media.

Challenges and Triumphs: Navigating the Literary World

Like many authors, Clarke faced challenges along the way. She has been open about her experiences with health issues, including chronic illness, and how they have shaped her creative process. Despite these obstacles, she has built a career marked by perseverance and adaptability. Clarke's ability to blend humor, suspense, and social commentary in her work sets her apart as a unique voice in modern British literature.

Legacy and Influence: A Voice for the Modern Era

Angela Clarke's novels have struck a chord with readers who are drawn to stories that reflect the complexities of contemporary society. Her exploration of the intersection between technology and crime has made her thrillers both timely and thought-provoking. As she continues to write across genres, her influence in both the literary and media worlds continues to grow.

Conclusion: A Creative Force Across Mediums

Angela Clarke's journey from fashion columnist to bestselling crime writer reflects her versatility and creativity. Whether writing thrillers, plays, or screenplays, Clarke's work explores the complexities of modern life with wit, insight, and suspense. Her ability to navigate multiple creative fields, along with her resilience in the face of challenges, makes her a role model for aspiring writers. Clarke's influence is a reminder that the best stories are those that reflect the world around us—and challenge us to think about it differently.

Alex Mercer's Success Story: The Father of Modern Marketing

"Using YouTube isn't just about uploading videos; it's about creating a gateway where every clip invites viewers into your world and every interaction turns them into a community." — ALEX MERCER, YOUTUBE STRATEGY EXPERT

Alex Mercer is a renowned YouTube strategy expert, celebrated for helping individuals and brands harness the power of video to build meaningful connections. Known for his belief that YouTube is more than a platform—it's a gateway to community building, Mercer's innovative approach has empowered countless creators to turn viewers into loyal communities. His journey from early struggles to becoming a recognized leader in the digital space highlights the value of persistence, creativity, and a deep understanding of audience engagement.

Early Life: A Passion for Storytelling and Technology

From a young age, Alex Mercer was drawn to storytelling and digital media. Growing up in the early days of the internet and the rise of platforms like YouTube, Mercer was fascinated by how videos could connect people across the world. He saw YouTube not just as a place to share content, but as a revolutionary medium for communication.

While attending college, Mercer experimented with making videos, but it wasn't the instant success he imagined. His early projects struggled to gain traction. However, rather than give up, Mercer devoted himself to understanding YouTube's algorithms, analytics, and audience behaviors, determined to crack the code of digital engagement.

Breaking Through: Becoming a YouTube Strategist

After learning the intricacies of SEO, content optimization, and community interaction, Mercer launched his own channel with a focus on niche content. By testing various formats and approaches, he discovered that consistent content, audience interaction, and strategic use of thumbnails and tags were the keys to growth. Mercer's channel began to thrive, attracting subscribers who appreciated his practical tips and engaging personality.

Soon, others started to take notice. Creators and small businesses reached out to Mercer for advice on how to grow their own channels. His ability to analyze trends and customize strategies for different niches earned him a reputation as an expert in YouTube growth and strategy.

Building a Brand: Consulting and Community Building

Recognizing a growing demand for YouTube expertise, Mercer launched his own consulting business, helping influencers, brands, and entrepreneurs build successful online presences. His philosophy, captured in the quote: *"Using YouTube isn't just about uploading videos; it's about creating a gateway where every clip invites viewers into your world and every interaction turns them into a community,"* became the foundation of his strategy. For Mercer, success on YouTube is not just about views but about engaging with viewers and building a sense of belonging.

He began offering courses, webinars, and one-on-one consultations, sharing his knowledge with others and guiding them on how to create content that resonates. His workshops emphasized authenticity, consistency, and community engagement, inspiring both new and established creators.

Overcoming Challenges and Embracing New Trends

Like many in the digital space, Mercer faced challenges as YouTube's algorithms evolved. Staying ahead of these changes required constant learning and adaptation. Mercer embraced new trends such as short-form content through YouTube Shorts and integrated social media strategies across platforms like Instagram and TikTok to complement his clients' YouTube channels.

Mercer's ability to innovate and adapt kept him at the forefront of the industry. Whether working with influencers, small businesses, or large corporations, he emphasized the importance of genuine connections over mere subscriber counts.

Legacy and Influence: Empowering Creators Worldwide

Today, Alex Mercer is regarded as one of the most influential YouTube strategists in the industry. His clients have collectively achieved millions of subscribers and billions of views, but Mercer takes the most pride in helping creators build communities that thrive both on and off the platform.

Mercer's influence extends beyond YouTube—he has become a sought-after speaker at conferences, sharing insights on digital marketing, content creation, and personal branding. His practical, actionable advice resonates with creators looking to build meaningful relationships with their audiences.

Conclusion: A Gateway to Success and Community

Alex Mercer's journey from struggling YouTuber to expert strategist exemplifies the power of persistence, adaptability, and community-driven growth. His approach to YouTube reflects a deep understanding of the platform's potential to foster connections and create opportunities for anyone with a story to share.

As YouTube continues to evolve, Mercer's influence remains at the cutting edge of digital strategy, reminding creators that every upload is an opportunity to invite viewers into a shared world. His story is an inspiration to anyone who believes in the transformative power of content, community, and connection.

CHAPTER TWO

Turning Goals into Reality

Success in business is rarely a stroke of luck—it's the result of meticulous planning, strategic thinking, and consistent execution. While vision serves as the guiding star, a well-thought-out plan acts as the map that turns ambitious ideas into actionable steps. A solid business plan provides the framework needed to navigate uncertainty, tackle challenges, and chart a sustainable path forward. As Daniel Kahneman, renowned psychologist and author of *Thinking, Fast and Slow*, emphasizes, effective decision-making requires thoughtful analysis and planning, allowing businesses to manage risks and seize opportunities with confidence.

Planning for success involves more than just setting goals—it's about turning those goals into detailed strategies that address every area of your business, from operations to marketing, finance, and growth. In this chapter, we explore how leaders like J. J. Abrams, master of long-term storytelling, use structured planning to transform abstract ideas into fully realized projects. Abrams's ability to meticulously map out narratives while leaving space for creative twists offers a powerful analogy for business planning: structure must coexist with flexibility.

Successful plans allow room for unexpected changes, ensuring that businesses can pivot when needed without losing sight of their long-term objectives.

As Jay Conrad Levinson, author of *Guerrilla Marketing*, teaches, strategy is also about identifying your edge—deliberately choosing a unique market position to stand out. Planning requires focusing on the right opportunities, customers, and markets, just as Levinson's unconventional tactics allowed small businesses to outperform competitors with larger budgets. Business plans must reflect these deliberate choices, pinpointing where and how a company will succeed.

However, planning isn't only about external strategy—it's also about internal preparation. Writers like Margaret Atwood, known for their ability to create complex worlds, demonstrate the power of thoughtful planning to maintain creative control over ambitious projects. Atwood's approach reminds us that business planning is not just about setting goals but building frameworks that empower teams to execute them effectively, while still allowing space for creativity and innovation along the way.

Similarly, Don Draper, the iconic advertising executive from *Mad Men*, exemplifies the importance of balancing bold ideas with disciplined planning. Draper's campaigns were rooted in clear strategies, yet they succeeded because they tapped into emotional connections. A strong business plan integrates data-driven analysis with compelling storytelling, turning strategic decisions into narratives that inspire employees, customers, and investors alike.

Another essential aspect of planning is agility and resilience. Jamie Thomas, known for reshaping the skateboarding industry, shows how adaptability is critical when navigating changing markets. The most successful businesses build strategies that allow for iterations and adjustments, much like Thomas's career, which evolved with each shift in trends. Flexibility within a plan ensures that your business can respond to unexpected developments without losing momentum.

Financial planning also plays a crucial role in turning goals into reality. As Evelyn Hart, a leader in the nonprofit sector, demonstrates, managing resources effectively is essential for any organization's long-term success. Whether through budgeting, cash flow projections, or risk management, a well-planned financial strategy reduces uncertainty and ensures that your business can weather challenges. As Kahneman warns, "Uncertainty is unavoidable, but smart planning reduces its impact." Understanding the financial side of your business equips you to make informed decisions and gives you the confidence to act with precision.

A well-designed plan also includes setting measurable goals. Like Susan Cooper, a master of weaving timelines and milestones into intricate narratives, business leaders must develop frameworks that keep their teams on track. Setting clear KPIs (Key Performance Indicators), creating realistic timelines, and breaking down long-term goals into smaller, actionable steps ensures steady progress. Monitoring these metrics and refining your approach along the way keeps your business aligned with its evolving objectives.

By the end of this chapter, you'll understand how to transform ambitious goals into actionable strategies. From crafting detailed business plans to managing financial risks, we'll provide you with the tools you need to build a roadmap for success. You'll also discover how to stay agile in the face of change, ensuring your plan evolves alongside your business.

Planning is not just about launching a business—it's about building an enterprise capable of thriving in any market condition. Whether through financial strategies, operational frameworks, or creative pivots, the leaders in this chapter—like Atwood, Draper, and Abrams—demonstrate that success lies in the intersection of discipline and imagination. With a strong plan in place and the flexibility to adjust course, you won't just reach your goals—you'll build a legacy that endures.

Daniel Kahneman's Success Story: The Psychologist Who Revolutionized Behavioral Economics

"Analyzing your launch isn't just about counting successes or failures; it's about decoding the data to strategically forge your path forward."
— DANIEL KAHNEMAN, PSYCHOLOGIST AND NOBEL
LAUREATE IN ECONOMIC SCIENCES

Daniel Kahneman is a world-renowned psychologist and Nobel laureate, known for transforming how we understand human decision-making through his pioneering work in behavioral economics. Kahneman's groundbreaking research has revealed the cognitive biases that shape our decisions, challenging the traditional assumption that people act rationally. His influence spans psychology, economics, and policy-making, helping organizations and governments design better systems by accounting for human error and irrationality.

Early Life: A Childhood Shaped by War

Daniel Kahneman was born on March 5, 1934, in Tel Aviv, Israel, but grew up in Paris, France. His early life was marked by upheaval and hardship. As a Jewish child during World War II, he experienced the horrors of the Holocaust firsthand. These traumatic experiences shaped Kahneman's interest in human behavior and the psychology of survival, laying the groundwork for his future research.

After the war, Kahneman and his family moved to British-controlled Palestine. He later pursued studies in psychology and philosophy at the Hebrew University of Jerusalem, graduating in 1954. His education and early interest in how people think and behave under pressure led him to explore cognitive psychology, a field that would define much of his career.

Academic Career: Laying the Foundations of Cognitive Psychology

Kahneman began his academic career as a researcher and lecturer at the Hebrew University, where he focused on perception and attention. His curiosity about how people interpret and respond to information evolved into a deeper interest in judgment and decision-making.

In the 1960s, Kahneman spent time at institutions in the United States, including Princeton University and the University of Michigan, where he continued to explore human cognition. During these years, Kahneman began to develop ideas about how intuitive thinking—the kind of quick, gut-feeling judgments people make—differs from analytical reasoning.

Collaboration with Amos Tversky: A Groundbreaking Partnership

Kahneman's most influential work emerged from his collaboration with fellow psychologist Amos Tversky. The two researchers began working together in the late 1960s and early 1970s, developing the prospect theory—a model explaining how people make decisions involving risk and uncertainty. They found that people are not perfectly rational; instead, they tend to overweight losses and underestimate gains, leading to irrational choices.

Their research also identified cognitive biases such as anchoring, availability heuristics, and loss aversion, which influence people's decisions without them realizing it. For example, people tend to rely heavily on the first piece of information they encounter (anchoring) or make decisions based on how easily examples come to mind (availability heuristic). These insights challenged the assumptions of traditional economics, which assumed that people act rationally to maximize their benefits.

The Nobel Prize: Recognition and Impact on Economics
In 2002, Kahneman was awarded the Nobel Memorial Prize in Economic Sciences for his work in behavioral economics. Although Tversky had passed away in 1996 and could not share the prize, Kahneman acknowledged that their work was a joint achievement. Kahneman's Nobel Prize was significant because it recognized psychology's contribution to economics, paving the way for new fields like behavioral finance and nudge theory.

Kahneman's research fundamentally changed how economists, businesses, and governments think about decision-making. It showed that human behavior is often irrational, but predictably irrational, allowing economists and policymakers to design better systems and interventions.

Beyond Academia: Books and Public Influence
In 2011, Kahneman published "Thinking, Fast and Slow," a bestselling book that summarizes his research and insights into human thinking. The book introduces the concept of System 1 and System 2 thinking:

- System 1 is fast, automatic, and intuitive.

- System 2 is slower, more deliberate, and analytical.

"Thinking, Fast and Slow" became a global phenomenon, praised for its accessible explanation of complex psychological concepts. It has influenced fields as diverse as business, economics, healthcare, and public policy, making Kahneman's insights widely applicable beyond academia.

Influence on Behavioral Economics and Policy

Kahneman's work laid the foundation for behavioral economics, which examines how psychological factors affect economic decision-making. His insights have had a profound impact on policy-making, influencing how governments design systems to encourage better decisions in areas like healthcare, retirement savings, and environmental conservation.

Behavioral economists, inspired by Kahneman's work, have developed nudge policies—small interventions that encourage people to make better choices without limiting their freedom. For example, automatically enrolling employees in retirement savings plans increases participation rates, reflecting how small changes can align behavior with long-term goals.

Awards and Continued Contributions

In addition to the Nobel Prize, Kahneman has received numerous honors, including the Presidential Medal of Freedom in 2013. Despite being officially retired, he continues to engage with researchers, policymakers, and the public. Kahneman remains an influential voice in both psychology and economics, emphasizing the importance of understanding human limitations to design better systems.

Legacy: A New Understanding of Human Nature

Daniel Kahneman's contributions have reshaped the way we think about decision-making, judgment, and behavior. His work has influenced economists, policymakers, and business leaders, leading to more effective solutions to complex challenges. Kahneman's insights into cognitive biases have made him one of the most influential thinkers of our time.

Conclusion: A Life of Inquiry and Discovery

Daniel Kahneman's journey from a young boy in war-torn Europe to a Nobel laureate reflects a lifetime of inquiry, curiosity, and collaboration. His ability to challenge conventional wisdom and provide new frameworks for understanding human behavior has had a lasting impact on psychology, economics, and public policy. Kahneman's story is a testament to the power of intellectual curiosity and the importance of exploring the complexities of human thought to create a better world.

J. J. Abrams's Success Story: Master of Mystery, Film, and Television

"Subsidiary rights are not just icing on the cake—they are layers of potential that can elevate a book from a single story to a multimedia franchise."
— J. J. ABRAMS, FILMMAKER AND PRODUCER

J. J. Abrams, an influential writer, director, and producer, has built a career at the intersection of storytelling and spectacle, bringing imaginative worlds to life on both the big and small screens. From hit TV shows like *Lost* to blockbuster franchises like *Star Wars* and *Star Trek*, Abrams has become known for blending sci-fi, drama, and mystery, captivating audiences worldwide. His success is rooted in a passion for storytelling, a talent for visual spectacle, and a deep understanding of character-driven narratives.

Early Life: A Passion for Stories and Film
Jeffrey Jacob Abrams was born on June 27, 1966, in New York City and raised in Los Angeles, where he was surrounded by the entertainment industry. His parents, Carol and Gerald Abrams, both worked in television, which sparked J. J.'s interest in film and storytelling from a young age. Abrams began experimenting with filmmaking as a child, using Super 8 cameras to shoot home movies, igniting a lifelong fascination with storytelling through visual media.

While studying at Sarah Lawrence College, Abrams worked on film projects, further honing his skills in writing and directing. One of his early breaks came while still in college—he was hired to write the screenplay for Taking Care of Business (1990), a comedy starring Jim Belushi. Although not yet recognized as a star in Hollywood, this project marked Abrams' entry into the entertainment industry.

Breaking into Television: Alias and Lost
Abrams began his television career in earnest by co-creating Alias (2001), an action-packed spy drama starring Jennifer Garner. With its mix of espionage,

family drama, and romance, *Alias* showcased Abrams' knack for blending genres. The show became a hit, earning both critical acclaim and a devoted fan base.

Building on the success of *Alias*, Abrams co-created Lost (2004) with Damon Lindel of, a series that would become one of the most influential TV dramas of the 21st century. *Lost* followed the survivors of a plane crash on a mysterious island, mixing science fiction, fantasy, and human drama. Abrams' signature use of mystery and intrigue kept viewers hooked, and *Lost* became a cultural phenomenon, redefining what television storytelling could achieve.

Making the Leap to Blockbuster Films: Mission: Impossible and Star Trek
After establishing himself as a television powerhouse, Abrams transitioned into blockbuster filmmaking. In 2006, he directed Mission: Impossible III, starring Tom Cruise. His ability to combine intense action sequences with emotional character moments reinvigorated the franchise and marked Abrams' arrival as a Hollywood director.

In 2009, Abrams took on a major challenge—revitalizing the Star Trek franchise with a reboot that appealed to both longtime fans and new audiences. His version of *Star Trek* introduced a younger cast and blended character-driven storytelling with dazzling special effects, earning both commercial and critical success. Abrams' work on *Star Trek* solidified his reputation as a director capable of balancing nostalgia with innovation.

Star Wars: Taking on a Legacy
In 2015, Abrams was entrusted with one of the most beloved franchises in cinematic history—Star Wars. He directed Star Wars: The Force Awakens, the first film in the sequel trilogy, and co-wrote the screenplay. *The Force Awakens* was a massive commercial success, earning over $2 billion worldwide. Abrams carefully honored the legacy of the original trilogy while introducing new characters and storylines, rekindling excitement among fans.

Abrams returned to the Star Wars universe to direct the final film in the trilogy, The Rise of Skywalker (2019), bringing the saga to a close. His ability to balance spectacle with emotional storytelling helped shape a new era for the franchise.

Mystery Box Philosophy: The Power of Intrigue
One of Abrams' defining creative philosophies is his concept of the "mystery box." He believes that mystery and curiosity are essential to storytelling, compelling audiences to keep watching or reading. Whether it's a mysterious island in *Lost* or the identity of Rey's parents in *Star Wars*, Abrams often incorporates unresolved questions into his stories, creating anticipation and encouraging speculation among audiences.

This approach has become a hallmark of Abrams' work, but it has also drawn some criticism. While fans appreciate the intrigue, some have expressed frustration when certain plot points remain unresolved or ambiguous.

Founding Bad Robot: A Creative Powerhouse
In 2001, Abrams founded Bad Robot Productions, a company that has become one of the most successful production houses in Hollywood. Bad Robot has produced hit films and TV shows, including *Cloverfield, Westworld, Super 8*, and *Fringe*. Through Bad Robot, Abrams has nurtured new talent and expanded his creative reach across genres.

Bad Robot has also been active in philanthropy and social initiatives, supporting education and diversity programs. Abrams' leadership at Bad Robot reflects his commitment to innovation and collaboration, fostering an environment where new ideas and perspectives thrive.

Challenges and Evolution: Navigating Success and Criticism
While Abrams' career has been filled with successes, he has faced challenges along the way. Some projects, including the later seasons of *Lost*, have been criticized for narrative complexity and unresolved plotlines. Similarly, his Star Wars films received mixed reactions, with fans debating the balance between nostalgia and originality.

Despite these challenges, Abrams has shown a remarkable ability to learn from feedback and adapt his creative process. His focus on storytelling, innovation, and collaboration has kept him at the forefront of the entertainment industry.

Legacy and Influence: A Storyteller for the Modern Era
J. J. Abrams has redefined what it means to be a storyteller in the 21st century, bridging the worlds of television, film, and digital media. His projects have not

only entertained millions but have also shaped how stories are told in an era of multiplatform entertainment. Abrams' influence extends beyond his work—his success has inspired new generations of filmmakers to pursue bold ideas and blend genres.

Conclusion: A Visionary at the Forefront of Entertainment

J. J. Abrams' journey from aspiring filmmaker to Hollywood powerhouse is a testament to the power of imagination, hard work, and resilience. His ability to create stories that resonate emotionally while captivating audiences with mystery has made him one of the most influential figures in entertainment.

Through his work at Bad Robot, Abrams continues to push the boundaries of storytelling, shaping the future of both film and television. Whether on the bridge of the Starship Enterprise or in a galaxy far, far away, Abrams' legacy will endure, reminding us that the best stories are those that make us wonder, feel, and dream.

Jay Conrad's Success Story: The Father of Guerrilla Marketing

"Direct marketing with flyers and postcards isn't just about reaching out—it's about touching people with a tangible piece of your brand that they can feel, keep, and remember." — JAY CONRAD LEVINSON, FATHER OF GUERRILLA MARKETING

Jay Conrad Levinson (1933–2013) revolutionized the world of marketing with his innovative "Guerrilla Marketing" concept, which focused on unconventional tactics that yield big results with minimal investment. Levinson's pioneering approach reshaped how small businesses and entrepreneurs market their products, empowering them to compete against larger corporations using creative, low-cost strategies.

Early Career: A Foundation in Advertising

Levinson's journey began in the world of traditional advertising. After studying psychology at the University of Colorado, he built a career in high-profile agencies like Leo Burnett in London and J. Walter Thompson in the United States.

Levinson worked on several iconic campaigns, contributing to memorable branding efforts such as the Marlboro Man, Tony the Tiger, and United Airlines' "Fly the Friendly Skies."

While these campaigns brought commercial success, Levinson recognized that small businesses, with limited budgets, struggled to compete using traditional advertising methods. This realization drove him to explore non-traditional marketing techniques that could provide high impact at a low cost.

The Birth of Guerrilla Marketing

In 1984, Levinson published "Guerrilla Marketing," a groundbreaking book that introduced his ideas to the world. His concept encouraged businesses to focus on creativity, customer relationships, and grassroots strategies rather than expensive advertising. Levinson's message resonated with small businesses, providing them with practical methods to build brand awareness and drive growth.

The success of *Guerrilla Marketing* led to a series of follow-up books and workshops, establishing Levinson as a leading authority in the marketing industry. His books have sold over 21 million copies and have been translated into 62 languages, becoming essential reading for entrepreneurs and MBA students worldwide.

A Legacy of Influence

Levinson's impact extended far beyond publishing. He founded the Guerrilla Marketing Association to coach businesses on implementing his techniques, and his work continues to inspire entrepreneurs and marketers globally. His strategies remain relevant in the digital age, with guerrilla marketing evolving to incorporate social media and viral campaigns.

Even today, Levinson's philosophy—"Marketing is every bit of contact your company has with anyone in the outside world"—continues to shape modern marketing practices, emphasizing that creativity and relationship-building are more important than massive budgets.

Conclusion: Transforming Marketing for Small Businesses

Jay Conrad Levinson's story is one of innovation, insight, and empowerment. His ability to rethink marketing from the perspective of small businesses allowed him to democratize marketing, giving smaller companies a chance to thrive. His legacy as the Father of Guerrilla Marketing endures, proving that success in business doesn't always require big spending—just big ideas and a commitment to building relationships.

Margaret Atwood's Success Story: A Literary Icon and Visionary

"Mastering file preparation for both electronic and print formats ensures your book always presents its best version, no matter the medium. It's the behind-the-scenes magic that makes your published work shine."
— MARGARET ATWOOD, CELEBRATED AUTHOR

"Revising your manuscript is like preparing for a grand performance. Every edit sharpens your story, ensuring it resonates with the audience long after the curtain falls." — MARGARET ATWOOD, AUTHOR

"Editing is the final, essential layer of magic that transforms your manuscript from a diamond in the rough to a polished, sparkling gem ready for its debut." — MARGARET ATWOOD, AWARD-WINNING AUTHOR

Margaret Atwood is one of the most celebrated authors of contemporary literature, known for her poetry, novels, and essays that explore themes of power, gender, environmentalism, and human rights. Her work spans multiple genres—science fiction, historical fiction, speculative fiction, and dystopia—and her insights have resonated across generations. Atwood's mastery of storytelling and her ability to comment on the pressing issues of her time have made her not just a literary icon but also a cultural force.

Early Life: A Childhood Rooted in Nature and Books
Margaret Eleanor Atwood was born on November 18, 1939, in Ottawa, Canada, and spent much of her childhood in the forests of northern Quebec, where her father worked as an entomologist. With limited access to formal education during those early years, Atwood developed a love for reading and writing at an early age, immersing herself in myths, fairy tales, and classic literature.

Her family eventually settled in Toronto, and Atwood went on to study at the University of Toronto, earning a Bachelor's degree in English. She later pursued graduate studies at Radcliffe College in Cambridge, Massachusetts, where she began to develop the analytical and literary skills that would shape her career.

Early Career: Poetry and the Rise to Fame

Atwood began her writing career as a poet. Her first collection, *Double Persephone* (1961), was privately printed and received critical attention. By the late 1960s, she had become part of the Canadian literary scene, earning national acclaim for collections like The Circle Game (1966), which won the Governor General's Literary Award.

While Atwood found initial success as a poet, it was her shift to novels and prose that propelled her to international fame. Her first novel, The Edible Woman (1969), was a satirical exploration of gender roles, anticipating many of the feminist themes she would develop throughout her career.

Breakthrough with *The Handmaid's Tale*

In 1985, Atwood published what would become her most famous novel, The Handmaid's Tale. The story, set in a dystopian future where women's rights are stripped away, is a powerful critique of patriarchy, authoritarianism, and religious extremism.

Although the novel was controversial at the time of its release, it quickly gained critical acclaim and became a modern classic. It won several awards, including the Arthur C. Clarke Award, and has been translated into more than 40 languages. In 2017, *The Handmaid's Tale* was adapted into an award-winning television series, bringing Atwood's work to new audiences and making the story even more relevant in the context of modern political movements.

Environmentalism and Speculative Fiction

Atwood has long been interested in environmental and social issues, themes that she explores in her speculative fiction novels. The MaddAddam Trilogy—comprising *Oryx and Crake* (2003), *The Year of the Flood* (2009), and *MaddAddam* (2013)—examines the consequences of genetic engineering, environmental collapse, and societal disintegration.

These works reflect Atwood's belief in the power of speculative fiction to comment on contemporary issues. She often insists that her novels, though imaginative, are grounded in real scientific and social trends—things that could happen in the near future if humanity doesn't change course.

Awards and Recognition

Throughout her career, Atwood has received numerous accolades, including the Booker Prize, which she won twice—first for The Blind Assassin (2000) and later for The Testaments (2019), the sequel to *The Handmaid's Tale*. She has also been awarded the Governor General's Award and the Golden Booker, which celebrates the best work in the prize's 50-year history.

Atwood's work goes beyond fiction; she is also known for her essays, critical commentary, and activism. She has been a vocal advocate for women's rights, environmental conservation, and freedom of speech, using her platform to promote social change.

Conclusion: A Voice for the Present and Future

Margaret Atwood's career is a testament to the power of storytelling to shape culture and provoke thought. Her ability to blend literary excellence with political and social insight has made her one of the most influential writers of the modern era. Atwood's works, particularly *The Handmaid's Tale*, remain deeply relevant today, continuing to inspire discussions on gender, power, and freedom.

As Atwood herself once remarked, "A word after a word after a word is power." Through her words, she has shaped literature and influenced the way we think about the future of humanity, making her a literary icon whose legacy will endure for generations.

———————

Don Draper's Success Story: The Art of Advertising and the Price of Reinvention

"Great ads don't just catch your eye; they captivate your imagination and compel you to act. That's the artistry of visuals that truly convert."
— DON DRAPER, CREATIVE DIRECTOR AND
ADVERTISING EXECUTIVE

Don Draper is a fictional character from the TV series *Mad Men* (2007–2015). As the Creative Director and later a partner at Sterling Cooper Draper Pryce, Draper embodies the glamorous and ruthless world of 1960s advertising. His talent for creating emotionally compelling campaigns is captured by the quote, *"Great ads don't just catch your eye; they captivate your imagination and compel you to act. That's the artistry of visuals that truly convert."*

Early Career: From Troubled Origins to Madison Avenue

Born Dick Whitman, Draper grew up in poverty during the Great Depression. Seeking to escape his traumatic past, he assumes the identity of Don Draper during the Korean War. With this new identity, he reinvents himself and enters the advertising industry in New York City. His rise in the competitive world of advertising is driven by his ability to understand human desires and fears, transforming these insights into compelling ad campaigns.

The Art of Advertising: A Gift for Storytelling

Draper's genius lies in his ability to craft narratives that connect emotionally with consumers. His campaigns often evoke nostalgia, desire, and ambition, playing on deep-seated human needs. One of his defining moments is the Kodak "Carousel" pitch, where he uses the concept of memory and family to sell a product, leaving both clients and viewers emotionally moved.

Draper believes that advertising is about creating dreams, tapping into the aspirations of consumers to sell products and ideas. His visionary campaigns reflect the idealism of the 1960s while revealing the deeper insecurities of the era.

Challenges and Successes: A Life of Reinvention

Despite his professional success, Draper's personal life is marked by turmoil. He struggles with alcoholism, infidelity, and depression, often feeling trapped by the very image of success he projects. His journey reflects the dark side of ambition—the tension between public appearance and personal authenticity.

Throughout *Mad Men*, Draper must navigate changing cultural landscapes, adapting his strategies to meet new demands as advertising evolves. His ability to reinvent himself and his ideas keeps him at the top, even as societal norms shift around him.

Legacy: A Cultural Icon of Advertising

Don Draper's character embodies the allure and complexity of the advertising world. His quote about visuals captivating imagination reflects his philosophy that great advertising is about more than just catching attention—it must inspire action. Draper's story resonates as a reflection of the American Dream—an exploration of the pursuit of success and the cost of achieving it.

In the end, Draper's legacy is one of transformation—not just of the products he sells but of himself, as he navigates the challenges of identity, creativity, and human connection.

Evelyn Hart's Success Story: Redefining Art with AI and CGRT

"AI and CGRT are not just tools, they are the new paintbrushes for modern artists, allowing us to stretch the canvas of creativity beyond traditional boundaries into realms previously only imagined."
— EVELYN HART, DIGITAL ART INNOVATOR

Evelyn Hart is a visionary digital artist and innovator whose work pushes the boundaries of creativity through AI (artificial intelligence) and CGRT (computer-generated real-time technology). Known for her belief that "AI and CGRT are not just tools; they are the new paintbrushes for modern artists, allowing us to stretch the canvas of creativity beyond traditional boundaries into realms previously only imagined," Hart has become a trailblazer in the digital art movement, inspiring others to embrace technology in artistic expression.

Early Life: A Passion for Art and Technology

Evelyn Hart's journey began with a deep love for both art and technology. From a young age, Hart displayed an aptitude for drawing, painting, and design, while also nurturing a fascination with computers and coding. Growing up during the rise of digital media, she often explored ways to blend traditional techniques with emerging technologies.

Hart pursued formal education in fine arts and computer science, attending a university where she honed her skills in both creative and technical disciplines. During her studies, she became captivated by the idea of using AI and computer-generated art to expand the limits of traditional art forms. Inspired by artists like Refik Anadol and movements like generative art, Hart began experimenting with algorithms and interactive technologies to create immersive experiences.

Embracing AI and CGRT: A New Creative Path

Early in her career, Hart recognized the transformative potential of AI and CGRT. While many artists were skeptical of these tools, viewing them as a threat to traditional craftsmanship, Hart saw them as extensions of the creative process. She believed that just as painters used brushes and sculptors used chisels, digital artists could use AI and CGRT to bring new dimensions to their work.

Her first major project involved creating dynamic installations where artwork would evolve in real-time based on audience interaction and environmental data. These works blurred the line between art, technology, and performance, earning her recognition for her pioneering approach. Hart quickly gained a reputation for merging creativity with code, using machine learning algorithms to produce visuals that responded to human input.

Breakthrough Projects and Recognition

Hart's breakthrough came with a series of exhibitions where she showcased AI-generated landscapes that shifted based on real-world data, such as weather patterns or time of day. These projects captivated audiences, not only for their beauty but also for how they engaged viewers in interactive storytelling.

Her ability to integrate real-time technology with artistic vision led to collaborations with tech companies, galleries, and immersive art installations worldwide. She was soon commissioned to create digital experiences for festivals and public spaces, becoming a leader in the intersection of art and technology.

Challenges and Perseverance

While Hart's innovative approach garnered praise, she also faced resistance from the traditional art world. Some critics questioned whether works created with the help of algorithms could be considered true art. Undeterred, Hart continued to advocate for the role of technology in creative expression, participating in lectures, panels, and workshops to share her philosophy with others.

She emphasized that AI was not a replacement for human creativity but a collaborator, capable of generating ideas and possibilities that artists might not have otherwise explored. Hart's persistence paid off as digital art gained mainstream acceptance, and institutions began recognizing the artistic value of AI-driven works.

Legacy: Inspiring the Next Generation of Artists

Today, Evelyn Hart is a renowned figure in the digital art community. Her work continues to explore how AI and CGRT can unlock new forms of artistic expression, from interactive installations to immersive digital environments. She has inspired countless artists to embrace technology as a tool for creation, proving that art can evolve while staying true to its roots.

Through her workshops and collaborations, Hart nurtures the next generation of digital artists, encouraging them to experiment fearlessly and challenge traditional notions of what art can be. Her influence is evident not only in galleries and museums but also in virtual spaces, where her work bridges the gap between art and technology.

Conclusion: Pioneering Art in the Digital Age

Evelyn Hart's journey from a curious young artist to a digital art innovator exemplifies the power of vision, adaptability, and creativity. Her belief that AI and CGRT are the new paintbrushes of modern art has reshaped how the world views artistic expression in the digital age. Hart's legacy reminds us that creativity knows no bounds—it evolves with technology, opening doors to new realms of possibility.

Jamie Thomas' Success Story: Skateboarding Legend and Entrepreneurial Pioneer

"Social media is the modern-day storyteller's canvas—every post a brushstroke, every live session a masterpiece in the making. Use each platform to weave tales that not only capture attention but also hearts and minds."
— JAMIE THOMAS, SOCIAL MEDIA STRATEGIST

Jamie Thomas, a professional skateboarder, entrepreneur, and industry innovator, has become one of the most influential figures in skateboarding. Known for his fearless style, business acumen, and commitment to the culture of skateboarding, Thomas has shaped the sport both as an athlete and as the founder of Zero Skateboards. His journey from a determined young skater to a business mogul and cultural icon reflects the power of passion, perseverance, and entrepreneurial spirit.

Early Life: Passion for Skateboarding

Jamie Thomas was born on October 11, 1974, in Dothan, Alabama, far from the skateboarding meccas of California. Growing up in a small town, Thomas was drawn to skateboarding at a young age. In the 1980s, skateboarding was still an emerging subculture, and resources were limited, but Thomas quickly fell in love with the freedom and creativity the sport offered.

Skating the streets and developing his skills on homemade ramps, Thomas faced many challenges early in his career. With few skate parks or mentors in his hometown, he taught himself by watching skate videos and practicing relentlessly. At age 17, Thomas left Alabama and moved to California—the epicenter of skateboarding culture—determined to make a name for himself.

Breaking into the Skateboarding Scene

Arriving in California, Thomas struggled at first to find his place in the highly competitive skateboarding industry. However, his aggressive and innovative skating style soon caught the attention of skate companies. Known for taking on high-risk stunts and bold challenges, Thomas quickly became known as a skater willing to push the limits.

His breakthrough came when he joined Toy Machine Skateboards, where he featured in several influential skate videos, including "Welcome to Hell" (1996). His daring tricks—such as jumping down massive stair sets and rails—made him a fan favorite and earned him a reputation as one of the most fearless skaters of his generation.

Founding Zero Skateboards: A New Chapter

In 1996, Jamie Thomas took a significant risk by starting his own skate company, Zero Skateboards. At the time, the skateboarding industry was dominated by established brands, and launching a new company was a bold move. However, Thomas was driven by a vision to create a brand that reflected the raw and rebellious spirit of skateboarding.

Zero Skateboards quickly gained a following for its distinctive style and intense skate videos, with Thomas leading the charge. The company's video, "Thrill of It All" (1997), and the follow-up, "Dying to Live" (2002), showcased Thomas and his team performing high-stakes tricks, helping Zero become one of the most influential brands in skateboarding.

Thomas also founded Fallen Footwear in 2003, a skate shoe company that became a staple in the industry, known for its design and functionality tailored to skaters' needs.

Challenges and Resilience

Despite his success, Thomas faced numerous challenges along the way. Running a skate company required more than just creativity; it demanded business acumen and the ability to adapt to market changes. The financial pressures of maintaining Zero and Fallen Footwear, especially during the economic downturn of the 2000s, forced Thomas to make tough decisions.

In 2016, Thomas announced that Fallen Footwear would cease operations due to financial difficulties, a significant setback in his career. However, he remained committed to his vision, later reviving the brand and rebuilding it with a renewed focus on skater-owned businesses and sustainability.

A Legacy of Impact and Influence

Today, Jamie Thomas is recognized as one of the most influential figures in skateboarding. His career has not only shaped the skateboarding industry but also inspired countless skaters around the world. As both an athlete and an entrepreneur, Thomas has redefined what it means to succeed in skateboarding, proving that passion, hard work, and vision can overcome even the most daunting obstacles.

In addition to his business ventures, Thomas has mentored younger skaters, helping foster the next generation of talent. His commitment to the skateboarding community extends beyond the board—he remains actively involved in philanthropic efforts and supports skater-owned projects.

Conclusion: A Legacy of Innovation and Perseverance

Jamie Thomas' journey from a small-town skater to an industry leader and entrepreneur is a story of determination, risk-taking, and passion. His ability to balance creative expression with business savvy has left a lasting impact on skateboarding culture. Whether through Zero Skateboards, Fallen Footwear, or his own skating career, Thomas' legacy continues to inspire skaters worldwide. His story is a testament to the idea that success comes not just from talent, but from dedication, resilience, and a willingness to push boundaries.

Susan Cooper's Success Story: The Master of Myth and Fantasy Literature

"Engage, enlighten, encourage and especially . . . just be yourself! Social media is a community effort, everyone is an asset." — SUSAN COOPER, MARKETING EXPERT

Susan Cooper is a renowned British author best known for her young adult fantasy series, *The Dark Is Rising* Sequence. Her stories, which weave together elements of myth, folklore, and modern adventure, have captivated readers for decades. With her deep love of storytelling and an ability to blend the real world with the magical, Cooper has become one of the most influential voices in children's and fantasy literature.

Early Life: A Love for Stories and Learning

Susan Mary Cooper was born on May 23, 1935, in Burnham, England. Growing up during World War II, she found solace in books, developing an early passion for myths, legends, and classic literature. Cooper was an avid reader, drawn to British folklore and Arthurian legends, themes that would later play a crucial role in her writing.

Cooper attended Oxford University, where she studied English literature and became one of the first women to study under J.R.R. Tolkien and C.S. Lewis— two legendary figures in the fantasy genre. While Tolkien and Lewis's works left a lasting impression on her, Cooper would later develop her own distinctive voice, grounded in her love of history and myth.

Early Career: Journalism and Transition to Fiction

After graduating from Oxford, Cooper initially pursued a career in journalism. She worked for the Sunday Times in London under Ian Fleming, the creator of James Bond. Her time in journalism sharpened her skills in concise storytelling and character development—tools she would later use in her novels.

In the early 1960s, Cooper moved to the United States, where she focused more on creative writing. Her first novel, "Mandrake" (1964), was a contemporary work, but it was her interest in children's fantasy literature that would soon define her career.

The Dark Is Rising: A Defining Series

Cooper's breakthrough came with the publication of Over Sea, Under Stone (1965), the first book in what would become The Dark Is Rising Sequence. However, it wasn't until the release of the second novel, *The Dark Is Rising* (1973), that the series gained widespread recognition. The sequence, consisting of five books, draws heavily on Arthurian legends, Celtic mythology, and British folklore, pitting the forces of Light and Dark against each other in an epic battle.

The series was unique in its combination of ancient myths with contemporary settings. Its blend of realism and fantasy, as well as its complex themes of courage, loyalty, and destiny, resonated deeply with both young and adult readers. Cooper's poetic prose, combined with her intricate world-building, set a new standard for children's fantasy literature.

Awards and Recognition

The *Dark Is Rising Sequence* received critical acclaim, earning numerous awards. In 1974, The Dark Is Rising was a Newbery Honor Book, and the final book in the series, Silver on the Tree (1977), solidified Cooper's reputation as a master storyteller.

Her books continue to be celebrated for their timeless appeal, influencing subsequent generations of fantasy writers. In 2012, Cooper was awarded the Margaret A. Edwards Award for lifetime achievement in young adult literature, recognizing the lasting impact of *The Dark Is Rising Sequence*.

Challenges and Later Works

Throughout her career, Cooper faced the challenges common to many writers—balancing creative expression with commercial pressures. However, she remained committed to crafting stories with depth and meaning, refusing to compromise on quality.

In addition to *The Dark Is Rising Sequence*, Cooper has authored several other novels, plays, and picture books, including The Boggart (1993) and King of Shadows (1999). Her work explores themes such as identity, history, and the connection between the past and present.

Legacy: Inspiring Generations of Readers

Susan Cooper's influence extends beyond the literary world. Her works have been adapted for stage and screen, and her stories continue to inspire new generations of readers and writers. The themes of Light and Dark in her books remain relevant, offering timeless lessons about hope, bravery, and the power of storytelling.

Cooper's ability to merge mythology with modern settings has made her a pivotal figure in fantasy literature, earning her comparisons to her former mentors, Tolkien and Lewis. Yet, her distinct voice and imaginative vision ensure that her legacy stands firmly on its own.

Conclusion: A Life Dedicated to Storytelling

Susan Cooper's career is a testament to the enduring power of myth and imagination. Her ability to create stories that transport readers into magical realms while addressing universal themes has earned her a place among the greats of children's literature. With her works continuing to inspire readers around the world, Cooper's legacy as a storyteller and cultural bridge between past and present remains stronger than ever.

=========

CHAPTER THREE

Building a Strong Framework for Growth

Choosing the right business structure is one of the most critical decisions an entrepreneur will make, as it establishes the foundation for how your business operates, grows, and engages with stakeholders. John D. Rockefeller, a pioneer of modern business practices, demonstrated that the right structure can shape an organization's future and create lasting influence. From determining taxation to defining ownership rights, liability, and decision-making processes, your business structure must align with both your immediate needs and long-term goals. As Rockefeller's legacy illustrates, carefully designed frameworks are essential for sustainable success.

This chapter focuses on helping you select a business structure that supports both operational efficiency and strategic growth. Whether you choose a sole proprietorship, partnership, LLC, or corporation, each option offers distinct advantages and challenges. Leo Burnett, an advertising legend, built one of the most influential agencies by selecting a structure that empowered creativity while maintaining operational discipline. His success highlights the importance of aligning your structure with your company's mission and ensuring that every part of your enterprise works together seamlessly.

But choosing a structure is just the beginning—execution is where plans become reality. Carter Jennings, a master of strategy implementation, demonstrated how well-defined processes and workflows drive business success. As former CEO Jack Welch once said, "Good business structure is not just about the hierarchy; it's about creating an environment where every piece and every person knows exactly where they fit in the puzzle of success." Jennings's work reminds us that strategy execution involves translating vision into actionable steps, ensuring that team members, processes, and resources are aligned with shared goals.

Creating a culture of accountability is essential to successful execution. Michael E. Gerber, author of *The E-Myth Revisited*, emphasizes the importance of systems in business growth, stating that clear roles and responsibilities are essential for scaling operations. By establishing feedback loops, setting performance metrics, and empowering employees, your business can foster a culture where every individual understands how their contributions advance the organization's objectives. Just as Burnett's advertising empire thrived on collaboration, a business built on effective communication and accountability stays on course even when challenges arise.

Financial alignment is another key element of strategic execution. Tim Berry, a thought leader in business planning, teaches that understanding cash flow, profit distribution, and financial reporting is essential for sustainable growth. Your business structure affects capital flow, taxation, and relationships with investors, making financial transparency and efficiency critical. With the right systems in place, you can optimize performance while ensuring compliance with legal and financial obligations, just as Berry's frameworks have guided countless entrepreneurs toward success.

In today's fast-changing marketplace, adaptability is essential. As Lorelle VanFossen, a digital strategist, shows through her work, the ability to pivot and adjust your strategy when needed keeps your business competitive. Strategy execution isn't a one-time event—it requires ongoing monitoring, assessment, and refinement. Whether you're expanding into new markets, launching a product, or executing a marketing campaign, agility ensures that your business stays resilient in uncertain environments. Like Rockefeller's ability to evolve Standard Oil, or Lucas Montgomery's success in navigating shifting market dynamics, strategic flexibility can determine whether your business flourishes or fails.

By the end of this chapter, you'll have the tools and insights needed to choose the right business structure and execute your strategy effectively. Drawing inspiration from Rockefeller, Jennings, and Gerber, you'll learn how to align operations with goals, empower your team, and create a performance-driven culture. Financial expertise, strategic agility, and a well-chosen structure will position your business to thrive amid change. With the right framework in place, your business won't just grow—it will evolve into a resilient enterprise capable of achieving long-term success in any market.

John D. Rockefeller's Success Story: The Father of Modern Marketing

"Tax planning is an essential skill for any business leader. Effective tax strategy goes beyond mere compliance; it involves making proactive decisions that can significantly impact your company's financial health."
— JOHN D. ROCKEFELLER, AMERICAN BUSINESS MAGNATE

John D. Rockefeller was a visionary businessman and philanthropist whose career shaped the modern American economy. As the founder of Standard Oil and the world's first billionaire, Rockefeller revolutionized the oil industry, introducing efficiency, innovation, and corporate structure that set the foundation for modern capitalism. His journey from humble beginnings to becoming one of the wealthiest individuals in history is a story of ambition, strategy, and philanthropy.

Early Life: Humble Beginnings
John Davison Rockefeller was born on July 8, 1839, in Richford, New York, to William Avery Rockefeller, a traveling salesman, and Eliza Davison Rockefeller, a deeply religious and frugal woman. From a young age, Rockefeller was taught

the importance of hard work and discipline, as his family often struggled to make ends meet. His mother instilled in him a strong sense of saving, tithing, and charity, habits that would remain with him throughout his life.

In 1853, the family moved to Cleveland, Ohio, where Rockefeller attended high school and later enrolled in a business course at Folsom Mercantile College. At just 16 years old, he took his first job as an assistant bookkeeper—earning 50 cents a day—and quickly demonstrated exceptional financial skills, excelling at accounting and negotiation.

Entry into the Oil Industry: Identifying an Opportunity

In the 1850s, the discovery of oil in Pennsylvania sparked a new industry, with oil refineries springing up across the region. Rockefeller, sensing the potential for profit, entered the business in 1863 by investing in a small oil refinery with a partner. Recognizing the chaotic nature of the oil industry, he believed that organization and efficiency could unlock immense profits.

In 1870, Rockefeller co-founded the Standard Oil Company in Cleveland. At the time, refining crude oil into kerosene for lamps was one of the most profitable uses of oil, and Standard Oil quickly became a leader in refining and distribution.

Building an Empire: The Rise of Standard Oil

Rockefeller's genius lay in streamlining operations and reducing costs. He introduced vertical integration, controlling every aspect of the business—from oil production to transportation, refining, and retail distribution. By cutting out middlemen and negotiating favorable rates with railroads, Rockefeller was able to undercut his competitors, acquiring struggling refineries and expanding Standard Oil's influence.

Standard Oil's success was also driven by innovations in refining technology and strategic business practices. Rockefeller formed trusts, consolidating multiple companies under a single umbrella, which allowed him to control the industry and eliminate competition. By the 1880s, Standard Oil controlled about 90% of the U.S. oil market, making it one of the most powerful monopolies in history.

Challenges and Controversies: Trust-Busting and Public Backlash

As Standard Oil grew, Rockefeller became a controversial figure. Many viewed his business practices as ruthless, accusing him of driving competitors out of business through predatory pricing and secret deals. The company's dominance led to a growing backlash, and public opinion turned against Rockefeller, who was seen as the embodiment of corporate greed.

In 1911, the U.S. Supreme Court ruled that Standard Oil violated antitrust laws and ordered the company to be broken up into smaller companies. Ironically, the breakup increased Rockefeller's wealth, as the individual companies—like Exxon, Chevron, and Mobil—became highly profitable on their own, with Rockefeller holding shares in each.

Philanthropy and Legacy: A New Chapter
Despite his reputation as a ruthless businessman, Rockefeller spent the latter part of his life focused on philanthropy. Believing in the principle of "giving back," he donated much of his fortune to causes that reflected his values, including education, public health, and scientific research.

In 1901, he established the Rockefeller Institute for Medical Research (now Rockefeller University), which became a leader in biomedical research. He also founded the University of Chicago and the Rockefeller Foundation in 1913, which aimed to promote the well-being of humanity. His philanthropic efforts significantly advanced public health, including efforts to eradicate diseases like hookworm and yellow fever.

By the time of his death in 1937, Rockefeller had given away more than $500 million (equivalent to billions today), transforming philanthropy into a structured discipline that influenced future generations of wealthy individuals, including Bill Gates and Warren Buffett.

Legacy: The Father of American Capitalism
John D. Rockefeller's life embodies both the promise and pitfalls of American capitalism. On one hand, he transformed the oil industry through innovation, efficiency, and business acumen, creating one of the largest companies in history. On the other hand, his monopolistic practices led to public outcry and the rise of antitrust regulations.

Rockefeller's influence on both business and philanthropy remains significant today. His approach to vertical integration and cost-cutting continues to shape modern corporations, while his charitable foundations laid the groundwork for scientific, educational, and medical advancements that have benefited millions.

Conclusion: A Life of Ambition and Generosity

John D. Rockefeller's journey from a modest upbringing in rural New York to becoming the world's first billionaire is a story of relentless ambition, innovation, and strategic brilliance. Though his career was marked by controversy, Rockefeller's lasting impact on business and philanthropy demonstrates the complexity of his legacy. He reshaped industries, created lasting institutions, and exemplified both the power and responsibility of wealth, leaving behind a legacy that continues to influence capitalism and philanthropy today.

———

Leo Burnett's Success Story: The Advertising Genius Who Created Iconic Brands

"Launching your business is like a grand performance—every detail matters, and first impressions are everything." — LEO BURNETT, ADVERTISING LEGEND

"Make it simple. Make it memorable. Make it inviting to look at. Make it fun to read." — LEO BURNETT, LEGENDARY ADVERTISING EXECUTIVE

"Effective advertising does not just circulate information. It penetrates the public mind with desires and belief." — LEO BURNETT, FOUNDER OF LEO BURNETT COMPANY, INC.

Leo Burnett was a visionary ad man, the founder of Leo Burnett Worldwide, and the creative mind behind some of the most iconic brand mascots in history, including Tony the Tiger, the Marlboro Man, and the Pillsbury Doughboy. His career was marked by a relentless pursuit of originality, simplicity, and emotional storytelling, transforming the advertising industry by creating ads that connected deeply with everyday people. Burnett's legacy is a reminder that great ideas, when rooted in human insight, have the power to build unforgettable brands.

Early Life: Humble Beginnings

Born on October 21, 1891, in St. Johns, Michigan, Leo Burnett grew up in a small-town, middle-class family. His father owned a general store, and it was there that young Leo first learned the value of hard work and developed an interest in understanding what customers wanted. Watching his father interact with customers planted the seeds of empathy and storytelling—two skills that would later define Burnett's career in advertising.

Burnett graduated from the University of Michigan in 1914 with a degree in journalism. His first job was as a reporter and editor for a local newspaper, but it wasn't long before Burnett realized his passion lay in the world of business and marketing.

Entering the World of Advertising

Burnett's career in advertising began with a job as a copywriter at Cadillac Motor Company in Detroit. There, he honed his ability to craft persuasive messages and learned the importance of branding. His next role was with Erwin, Wasey & Company, an advertising agency where he gained experience in national ad campaigns.

However, Leo Burnett wasn't content working for someone else—he dreamed of starting his own agency, one that would break the mold and redefine advertising by focusing on simple, relatable storytelling.

The Birth of Leo Burnett Company

In 1935, in the midst of the Great Depression, Leo Burnett took a bold leap. With $50,000, part of it raised by pawning his wife's jewelry, Burnett founded the Leo Burnett Company in a small office in Chicago. On the first day of operation, Burnett famously placed a bowl of fresh red apples in the reception area—a subtle message to visitors that his agency believed in optimism, generosity, and creativity even in hard times.

Though the economy was in shambles, Burnett's vision was clear: his agency would focus on connecting with audiences emotionally, using simple but powerful ideas that resonated with everyday people.

Changing the Game: Creating Iconic Mascots

Burnett believed that advertising should focus on human emotions and experiences. He rejected flashy, complex ads and instead embraced "warm, friendly, and meaningful" concepts. Burnett's genius lay in his ability to personify brands, creating mascots and characters that made products instantly recognizable and memorable.

Some of his most iconic creations include:

- **The Marlboro Man**: Originally aimed at women, Marlboro cigarettes were repositioned for men with the rugged cowboy imagery of the Marlboro Man. This campaign became one of the most successful in history, helping Marlboro dominate the cigarette market for decades.

- **Tony the Tiger**: Burnett's team transformed Kellogg's Frosted Flakes into a beloved household name by creating the friendly, confident Tony the Tiger, with his famous tagline, "They're grrreat!"

- **The Pillsbury Doughboy**: With his giggle and pokeable belly, the Pillsbury Doughboy became an instantly recognizable symbol of warmth and home cooking.

- **The Jolly Green Giant**: This character turned Green Giant vegetables into a trusted, familiar brand.

These characters didn't just sell products—they created emotional connections with consumers, making them feel like the brands were part of their daily lives.

Burnett's Philosophy: "The Warmth of Human Kindness"

Leo Burnett was famous for saying, "When you reach for the stars, you may not get one, but you won't come up with a handful of mud either." His philosophy revolved around optimism, hard work, and creative ambition. Burnett believed that great advertising spoke to the heart, not just the mind, and he insisted that his agency's work reflect the warmth of human kindness.

Burnett also pioneered the idea of "inherent drama"—the belief that every product has a unique story waiting to be told. For Burnett, the job of an advertiser was to find the product's emotional core and communicate it in a way that captivated the audience.

Overcoming Challenges: Resilience in a Tough Industry
Burnett's journey wasn't without challenges. Launching a business during the Great Depression required resilience and tenacity. There were moments when his agency struggled to land clients, and the advertising industry itself was undergoing massive changes.

But Burnett's commitment to creativity and quality never wavered. He built a company culture that encouraged collaboration and bold ideas, earning the trust of major clients like Kellogg's, Procter & Gamble, and Philip Morris.

His ability to stay ahead of trends and adapt to the changing market helped the Leo Burnett Company grow into one of the largest advertising agencies in the world.

Leaving a Legacy: A Lasting Impact on Advertising
Leo Burnett remained actively involved in the agency until his retirement in the 1960s. By the time he stepped down, his agency was one of the most respected and successful in the industry, with a client roster that included some of the biggest brands in the world.

Even after his death in 1971, Burnett's influence continued to shape advertising. The agency he founded became Leo Burnett Worldwide, with offices around the globe. His approach to emotional storytelling, iconic mascots, and human connection remains a gold standard in modern advertising.

Key Lessons from Leo Burnett's Success

- **Find the human connection**: Burnett believed that the best ads were those that connected with people's emotions and experiences.

- **Embrace simplicity**: His campaigns focused on clear, meaningful storytelling, proving that simple ideas often have the greatest impact.

- **Build recognizable brands**: Through mascots and characters, Burnett made products memorable and relatable.

- **Stay optimistic**: Launching a business during the Great Depression taught Burnett the value of optimism and resilience.

- **Aim high**: Burnett's motto, "Reach for the stars," reflects his belief in the power of ambition and creativity.

Conclusion: A Legacy of Creativity and Heart

Leo Burnett's story is one of vision, persistence, and creativity. His ability to see the heart of a product and tell its story through characters and emotion revolutionized the advertising industry. Burnett's belief in the power of human connection and optimistic storytelling transformed the way companies communicate with their audiences, leaving behind a legacy that continues to inspire advertisers today.

Whether it's Tony the Tiger's roar, the Marlboro Man's rugged silhouette, or the Pillsbury Doughboy's giggle, Burnett's work lives on as a testament to the idea that great advertising is not just about selling—it's about building relationships that stand the test of time.

Carter Jennings' Success Story: Mastering the Alchemy of Video Production

"Great video production is like alchemy—it's part science, part art, blending visuals, sound, and editing into a masterpiece that transcends the medium itself." — CARTER JENNINGS, FILMMAKER AND EDITOR

Carter Jennings is a renowned filmmaker, editor, and visionary in video production, known for his ability to blend technical precision with creative storytelling. His work reflects a belief that great video production is like alchemy—part science, part art, blending visuals, sound, and editing into a masterpiece that transcends the medium itself. Jennings' career has been defined by his passion for storytelling through moving images, and he has become a sought-after figure in the industry for his ability to create emotionally resonant and visually stunning content.

Early Life: A Passion for Stories and Technology

From an early age, Carter Jennings was fascinated by the intersection of technology and art. Growing up with access to camcorders and editing software, he often spent hours experimenting with video, creating small films with friends, and learning to edit footage using early digital tools. His influences ranged from classic cinema to modern experimental filmmaking, and he developed a keen sense for how to use visual and audio elements to evoke emotion.

While in high school, Jennings worked on small video projects, gaining experience with lighting, camera work, and post-production editing. Encouraged by his teachers, he pursued his passion further by studying film production and media arts at university. During his college years, Jennings learned the science behind visual storytelling—from camera technology to sound design—while also developing his artistic voice.

Breaking into the Industry: Finding His Niche

After graduating, Jennings faced the challenges of breaking into the competitive film and video industry. He began by freelancing as a video editor, working on a variety of projects ranging from music videos and commercials to corporate content and independent short films. His early work showcased a talent for elevating seemingly simple projects into visually striking narratives.

As Jennings' reputation grew, he began collaborating with filmmakers, production houses, and media companies, gaining experience in cinematography, directing, and editing workflows. His versatility—being able to handle both technical aspects and creative direction—set him apart in the industry.

Crafting a Signature Style: The Alchemy of Storytelling

Jennings' approach to video production is rooted in his philosophy that art and science must work together to create compelling content. He is known for his ability to seamlessly blend visuals, music, and sound design, treating each project as a work of art that demands attention to both the technical details and emotional storytelling. Whether editing a fast-paced commercial or directing a heartfelt documentary, Jennings strives to connect with audiences on a deeper level.

One of his early breakthrough moments came when a music video he edited went viral, catching the attention of larger production companies. This led to more significant opportunities, including ad campaigns, branded content, and short films. His ability to capture authentic moments and enhance them through editing earned him recognition as a go-to editor and filmmaker for projects that needed to stand out.

Building a Brand and Business: Jennings Productions

As Jennings' profile grew, he founded Jennings Productions, a video production company specializing in high-quality visual storytelling. Through his company, he worked with clients from various industries, creating everything from corporate films to creative advertising campaigns. His team of filmmakers, editors, and sound designers shared his vision of merging creativity with technical precision.

Jennings also developed a reputation as a mentor, sharing his knowledge of video editing software, camera techniques, and storytelling frameworks with aspiring filmmakers. His workshops on blending creativity and technology in filmmaking attracted students, fellow filmmakers, and even established professionals looking to enhance their craft.

Overcoming Challenges: Evolving with the Industry

The world of filmmaking is constantly evolving, and Jennings understood the importance of adapting to new trends and technologies. From 4K video and drones to virtual production techniques and social media storytelling, Jennings embraced innovation, incorporating new tools to enhance his projects without losing sight of the core storytelling principles.

He also faced the challenge of keeping his creative work authentic and engaging in an industry increasingly dominated by content overload and shrinking attention spans. Jennings tackled this by focusing on quality over quantity, creating videos that resonate emotionally with viewers, rather than chasing trends.

Legacy and Influence: An Advocate for the Power of Video

Carter Jennings' work reflects the idea that video production is more than just assembling footage—it's an art form that requires mastery of every element, from visuals and sound to pacing and rhythm. His passion for storytelling through video has influenced not only his clients and collaborators but also the wider filmmaking community.

Jennings continues to inspire a new generation of filmmakers by emphasizing the importance of creativity and craft. He often speaks at industry events and conducts online courses, sharing his insights on how to balance technical skills with artistic vision.

Conclusion: A Master of Modern Filmmaking
Carter Jennings' story is one of passion, perseverance, and innovation. From his early days experimenting with cameras to becoming a leader in video production, Jennings has shown that success lies in blending art with science to create something greater than the sum of its parts. His ability to connect with audiences through visuals, sound, and editing continues to set him apart as a filmmaker and editor. Jennings' belief that video production is a modern form of alchemy reflects his commitment to elevating every project into a masterpiece that transcends the medium itself.

Michael E. Gerber's Success Story: The Visionary Behind Small Business Success

"Selecting the right business structure, be it a partnership or an LLC, is a foundational decision that defines both your financial journey and your strategic vision." — MICHAEL E. GERBER,
AUTHOR AND BUSINESS CONSULTANT

Michael E. Gerber is a renowned entrepreneur, author, and business coach, best known for his influential book, "The E-Myth Revisited: Why Most Small Businesses Don't Work and What to Do About It." His insights into the challenges facing small businesses and his practical frameworks for sustainable growth have made him a pioneer in business coaching. Gerber's success story is one of identifying systemic problems, creating scalable solutions, and helping millions of entrepreneurs transform their businesses.

Early Life: Discovering a Passion for Teaching and Business
Michael E. Gerber was born in California in 1936. Before entering the world of business coaching, Gerber explored a variety of jobs in industries ranging from music to sales, but it wasn't until later in life that he discovered his true calling—mentoring entrepreneurs. His early experiences working in sales gave him insight

into how businesses succeed and fail, particularly the challenges faced by small business owners.

In the 1970s, Gerber was invited to consult with a small business owner struggling to manage operations. He realized that many entrepreneurs knew their craft well but lacked the business systems needed to scale and sustain their enterprises. This moment sparked an idea that would become the foundation of his life's work.

The Birth of the E-Myth: Identifying the Entrepreneurial Myth

In 1977, Gerber founded E-Myth Worldwide, a company dedicated to helping small businesses grow through systematic processes and entrepreneurial coaching. The name "E-Myth" stands for the "Entrepreneurial Myth"—the false belief that technical expertise alone is enough to run a successful business. Gerber argued that many small businesses fail because their owners work in the business, focusing on day-to-day operations, rather than on the business, where they would develop strategies and systems for growth.

This insight became the cornerstone of Gerber's teachings, which emphasize that entrepreneurs must learn to delegate, create repeatable processes, and implement systems to achieve sustainable growth. Gerber's goal was to help business owners transition from being technicians to strategic thinkers, allowing their businesses to grow beyond their personal involvement.

Publishing *The E-Myth Revisited*: A Business Classic

In 1986, Gerber published the original edition of The E-Myth. The book's message resonated with readers, and in 1995, Gerber released an updated version titled The E-Myth Revisited, which became a global bestseller. The book provides a step-by-step guide to building a small business that can function independently of the owner's constant involvement.

The E-Myth Revisited introduced concepts such as:

- **The Technician, Manager, and Entrepreneur Roles** – Describing how every business owner must learn to balance these three identities to succeed.

- **Systemization** – Creating documented processes to ensure the business runs smoothly, even without the owner's direct involvement.

- **The Turn-Key Revolution** – Drawing inspiration from franchise models, Gerber emphasized building businesses with systems that allow them to scale effortlessly.

The book struck a chord with millions of business owners and became one of the most widely read business books of all time, earning a permanent place on entrepreneurship reading lists.

Building E-Myth Worldwide: Transforming Small Business Coaching
Following the success of *The E-Myth Revisited*, Gerber expanded his vision by building E-Myth Worldwide into a leading business coaching and consulting firm. He developed workshops, coaching programs, and courses, all designed to help small business owners implement the principles laid out in his book.

Through his coaching business, Gerber worked with thousands of entrepreneurs across industries, providing tailored advice to help them restructure their companies. His approach empowered business owners to focus on strategy, leadership, and systemization, enabling them to step out of day-to-day operations.

Challenges and Evolution: Adapting to a Changing Business Landscape
Although Gerber's E-Myth methodology proved immensely successful, he faced the challenge of adapting to a rapidly changing business environment. As the rise of digital tools and online businesses transformed how companies operate, Gerber continued to refine his methods to stay relevant. He embraced new technologies and digital platforms, offering online coaching and consulting to entrepreneurs around the world.

Throughout his career, Gerber remained committed to his core message—that systems, processes, and leadership are essential for building businesses that thrive long-term. His work has influenced countless entrepreneurs, business coaches, and consultants, shaping the modern business coaching industry.

Legacy and Continued Impact
Today, Michael E. Gerber is recognized as a thought leader in entrepreneurship, and his influence extends far beyond the pages of his books. The E-Myth Revisited has sold millions of copies worldwide and has been translated into multiple languages. It continues to be a go-to resource for small business owners seeking practical advice on building sustainable enterprises.

Gerber has also authored several other books, including The E-Myth Real Estate Investor, The E-Myth Chiropractor, and Awakening the Entrepreneur Within, expanding his teachings to niche industries. His ability to demystify the challenges of entrepreneurship and offer actionable solutions has made him a trusted mentor to business owners at all stages of their journeys.

Conclusion: A Legacy of Empowering Entrepreneurs

Michael E. Gerber's story is one of vision, persistence, and a passion for empowering others. From his early days consulting with struggling businesses to becoming one of the most influential business coaches in the world, Gerber has transformed the way entrepreneurs think about growth and sustainability. His insights into systemization and leadership have inspired millions of business owners to work smarter, not harder, building companies that thrive beyond the founder's involvement.

Gerber's legacy is not just in his books and coaching programs—it lives on in the thousands of businesses that have flourished by following his principles. His belief that anyone can build a successful business with the right systems and mindset remains as relevant today as when he first introduced the E-Myth philosophy, cementing his place as a pioneer in the world of entrepreneurship and business coaching.

Lorelle VanFossen's Success Story: Pioneering Education in Virtual Reality and Digital Storytelling

"Your blog is your unedited version of yourself." — LORELLE VANFOSSEN, A PROMINENT BLOGGER AND WORDPRESS AUTHORITY

Lorelle VanFossen is an innovator in digital storytelling, immersive education, and web publishing. As co-founder of Educators in VR, she has been at the forefront of integrating virtual reality (VR) and augmented reality (AR) into education, transforming how students, educators, and institutions engage with knowledge. Her career spans over 30 years, marked by groundbreaking contributions to the fields of VR education, digital content creation, and web technologies.

Early Life and Career: A Passion for Communication and Education
VanFossen's journey began with a deep passion for communication, education, and digital technologies. Early in her career, she became involved in blogging and digital publishing, establishing herself as an influential voice in the WordPress community. Her work focused on teaching individuals and businesses how to use digital platforms for storytelling and outreach, helping creators leverage new technologies to share their messages effectively.

VanFossen quickly earned a reputation for her ability to blend storytelling with technology. She contributed thousands of articles and conducted workshops on topics related to web publishing and online education, establishing herself as a leader in the digital education movement.

Founding Educators in VR: A Bold Vision for Immersive Learning
In 2018, VanFossen co-founded Educators in VR alongside Daniel Dyboski-Bryant, with the mission of bringing virtual and augmented reality into education. Their organization sought to transform learning by enabling educators to create immersive, engaging environments where students and teachers could connect regardless of geographic barriers. The platform fosters collaboration and innovation, empowering educators to explore new ways of teaching and interacting in virtual spaces.

VanFossen's work with Educators in VR culminated in the 2020 Educators in VR International Summit, a groundbreaking event that hosted 170 speakers across five virtual platforms, attracting more than 6,000 attendees from around the world. The summit was a milestone in immersive education, demonstrating how VR technology can enhance the learning experience by making it more interactive and accessible.

Challenges and Growth: Adapting to a Digital World
Throughout her career, VanFossen has navigated the evolving landscape of digital technologies, adapting her teaching methods to keep pace with advancements. As the world shifted toward remote learning during the COVID-19 pandemic, her expertise in virtual education proved invaluable. Educators in VR quickly became

a leading resource for schools and institutions transitioning to online and immersive education.

VanFossen has conducted over 1,000 workshops, keynotes, and training sessions, both in real-world and virtual environments, helping educators develop the skills they need to thrive in immersive teaching spaces. Her ability to inspire others to embrace new educational technologies has made her a prominent thought leader in digital education and immersive learning.

Legacy and Influence: A Lifelong Educator and Innovator

VanFossen's contributions extend beyond education into the broader field of digital storytelling and content creation. Her influence on web publishing has helped shape the careers of countless content creators, while her work with Educators in VR continues to inspire educators around the globe to think differently about teaching.

Her approach emphasizes that technology is a tool to foster deeper human connections. She believes that VR and AR can break down barriers between students and teachers, creating collaborative environments where learning becomes a shared experience.

Conclusion: Leading the Future of Education

Lorelle VanFossen's career exemplifies innovation, adaptability, and leadership in the evolving world of digital education and immersive learning. From her early work in web publishing to her pioneering efforts in VR education, VanFossen has consistently demonstrated the power of blending technology with storytelling to make a meaningful impact. Her legacy as a thought leader and educator will continue to shape how future generations learn, connect, and create in both virtual and physical spaces.

Tim Berry's Success Story: The Journalism to Business Planning Pioneer

"Good business planning is 9 parts execution for every 1 part strategy."
— TIM BERRY, BUSINESS PLANNING EXPERT

Tim Berry is a business planning expert, author, and entrepreneur, best known as the founder of Palo Alto Software and the creator of Business Plan Pro and LivePlan, two widely used business planning tools. His journey from journalism to software entrepreneurship exemplifies his ability to adapt, innovate, and guide others through the challenges of building a business.

Early Career: A Journalist's Start

Berry's career began in journalism. He worked as a night editor for UPI in Mexico City and as a correspondent for McGraw-Hill World News, contributing to publications like *BusinessWeek* and the *Financial Times*. His work in journalism provided him with writing, research, and analytical skills, which would later serve him well in the world of entrepreneurship and business planning.

Venturing into Software and Entrepreneurship

Berry's shift into entrepreneurship came when he recognized the need for practical business planning tools. In 1988, he founded Palo Alto Software, initially focusing on consulting. However, as the need for accessible business planning grew, Berry transitioned his company from a service model to a product-focused software company.

In 1994, Palo Alto Software released Business Plan Pro, which became a market leader in helping small businesses and startups develop detailed, effective business plans. Later, Berry and his team developed LivePlan, a cloud-based platform that makes business planning even more accessible and interactive.

Challenges and Growth: Building a Sustainable Company

Tim Berry's journey wasn't without challenges. During difficult financial times, Berry and his family faced significant personal debts, but through resilience and strategic growth, he managed to build his company into a successful business without relying on outside investors. By the time Berry stepped down from day-to-day operations, Palo Alto Software had achieved multi-million dollar sales and held 70% market share in its category.

Author, Educator, and Advocate for Lean Business Planning

Berry is also a prolific author, having written several influential books, including "The Plan-As-You-Go Business Plan" and "Lean Business Planning." His books emphasize agility and simplicity in business planning, promoting the idea that plans should be flexible, actionable, and regularly updated.

In addition to writing, Berry has taught entrepreneurship at the University of Oregon for over a decade and served as a mentor and judge at prominent business plan competitions. His practical insights into business planning have made him a sought-after speaker and mentor for entrepreneurs worldwide.

Legacy and Impact

Tim Berry's work has influenced millions of small business owners and entrepreneurs, providing them with tools and frameworks to start, manage, and grow their businesses. As a thought leader in business planning, Berry continues to share his expertise through blogs, webinars, and consulting, empowering new generations of entrepreneurs to think strategically and act with purpose.

Berry's ability to bridge the gap between creativity and business strategy has left a lasting impact on the entrepreneurial landscape, solidifying his reputation as the "Obi-Wan Kenobi of business plans."

Lucas Montgomery's Success Story: A Digital Publishing Trailblazer

"Mastering Amazon Kindle Programs is like unlocking a chest of digital possibilities, each tool a gem designed to bring your books into the hands of eager readers worldwide." — LUCAS MONTGOMERY, DIGITAL PUBLISHING EXPERT

Lucas Montgomery is a digital publishing expert known for helping authors and publishers master Amazon Kindle programs and navigate the complexities of self-publishing. With his strategic insight and practical approach, Montgomery has empowered countless writers to unlock new opportunities in the digital world. His quote, *"Mastering Amazon Kindle Programs is like unlocking a chest of digital possibilities, each tool a gem designed to bring your books into the hands of eager readers worldwide,"* encapsulates his passion for leveraging technology to democratize publishing.

Early Passion for Literature and Technology
Montgomery's love for books and technology started early. Growing up, he was an avid reader with a fascination for how digital platforms were transforming industries. This dual passion for storytelling and innovation would become the foundation of his career.

In college, Montgomery pursued a degree in media and communications, where he discovered the potential of e-books and online distribution. He recognized early on that Amazon's Kindle Direct Publishing (KDP) and other digital platforms were opening doors for independent authors, enabling them to reach a global audience without the need for traditional publishing.

Breaking into Digital Publishing
After graduation, Montgomery began working with independent authors and small publishers, helping them format and publish e-books on platforms like Amazon Kindle. He quickly became known for his in-depth understanding of the Kindle ecosystem—from navigating KDP tools and royalties to optimizing categories, keywords, and marketing strategies. His ability to simplify complex processes and offer practical advice made him a go-to resource for aspiring authors.

In 2015, Montgomery launched his own consulting business, focusing on digital publishing strategies. His workshops and online courses taught authors how to create, publish, and promote their books effectively. He also began offering personalized coaching, guiding authors through the intricacies of Amazon programs like KDP Select, Kindle Unlimited, and Kindle Promotions.

A Breakthrough with E-Book Marketing and Amazon Success
Montgomery's career took off when several of his clients' books became Amazon bestsellers, thanks to his strategic advice on marketing, pricing, and optimization. His innovative use of tools such as pre-orders, discounted promotions, and reader reviews helped authors boost visibility and increase sales. His success stories soon attracted larger publishing clients, and Montgomery's reputation as a digital publishing expert continued to grow.

In addition to his consulting work, Montgomery started publishing his own guides and courses, teaching authors how to build successful careers through self-publishing. His online courses covered everything from formatting e-books and running Amazon ads to mastering book launches and email marketing strategies.

Challenges and Adaptation in a Rapidly Changing Industry

The digital publishing world is constantly evolving, and Montgomery has stayed ahead of the curve by adapting to new trends. As Amazon introduced new tools and algorithms, he continually refined his strategies to help authors maximize their potential. He also expanded his expertise to cover emerging platforms such as Audible for audiobooks and IngramSpark for print-on-demand services.

Montgomery's approach emphasizes the importance of building a brand as an author, encouraging writers to engage with their readers through newsletters, social media, and personal websites. His ability to blend creative storytelling with practical business strategies has made him a trusted mentor in the indie publishing community.

Legacy and Influence in Digital Publishing

Today, Lucas Montgomery is recognized as one of the leading voices in self-publishing. His workshops, webinars, and consulting services continue to empower independent authors to take control of their publishing journeys. Through his guidance, countless writers have been able to publish successful books, build loyal followings, and turn their passions into sustainable careers.

Montgomery's philosophy—that digital publishing is a gateway to limitless possibilities—has inspired authors worldwide to embrace technology and innovation. His work reflects a deep belief that storytelling should be accessible to everyone, and that Amazon's Kindle ecosystem offers a powerful platform for authors to connect with readers across the globe.

Conclusion: Transforming Dreams into Digital Reality

Lucas Montgomery's journey from a passionate reader to a digital publishing pioneer is a story of adaptability, insight, and entrepreneurship. Through his mastery of Amazon's Kindle programs, he has helped authors unlock new opportunities and bring their stories to life. His legacy continues to shape the future of self-publishing, proving that with the right tools and strategies, anyone can find success in the digital publishing world.

CHAPTER FOUR

The Art of Developing a Standout Brand

In today's competitive world, personal branding has evolved from a buzzword into an essential tool for entrepreneurs, creatives, and business leaders. A well-defined personal brand is more than just a title or resume—it reflects who you are, what you stand for, and the distinct value you bring to the world. Your personal brand serves as your reputation, your identity, and your story, creating a bridge between you and your audience. As Shonda Rhimes, acclaimed television producer and creator, reminds us, "Your brand is not just what you say—it's the consistent story you tell through your actions." In this chapter, we explore how embracing personal branding can transform your career, business, and life trajectory.

Authenticity lies at the heart of successful personal branding. Shonda Rhimes built her empire by presenting a genuine version of herself, infusing her work with vulnerability and truth that resonates deeply with audiences. Personal branding is not about manufacturing a persona—it's about aligning your outward message with your inner values. Lisa Scottoline, bestselling author, emphasizes that authenticity breeds connection and trust. This chapter will guide you through the process of identifying your core values and using them to shape an authentic brand that aligns with both your personal and professional ambitions.

Your personal brand is also a powerful competitive advantage, especially in industries where products and services can appear indistinguishable. David Meerman Scott, marketing strategist and author, teaches that "Your brand is the emotional connection people feel when they encounter your name, product, or message." By leveraging your personal narrative, you can create a powerful story that forges emotional connections with customers, partners, and investors. This chapter will show you how every interaction—whether through public speaking, social media, or writing—is an opportunity to shape perceptions and build trust.

In the digital age, personal branding is more accessible—and necessary—than ever before. Rebecca Lieb, content marketing expert, advises, "Your digital presence is an extension of your personal brand—what you publish online shapes your professional identity." This chapter will walk you through the process of building a consistent online presence across platforms like LinkedIn, Instagram, and personal websites. You'll learn best practices for creating meaningful content, engaging with your audience, and maintaining authenticity with every post, ensuring that your brand message remains unified across all digital touchpoints.

Moreover, personal branding isn't just about external visibility—it's also a pathway to personal growth. Max Harmon, a business coach and strategist, emphasizes that defining your brand forces you to reflect on your strengths, areas of improvement, and long-term vision. This chapter will challenge you to align your personal goals with your business mission, creating a brand identity that reflects your purpose and inspires others to follow your journey. As Naomi Simmons, a leadership expert, reminds us, "People don't just buy what you sell—they buy why you do it."

Throughout this chapter, we'll provide actionable strategies to help you develop and enhance your personal brand. You'll learn how to craft a compelling elevator pitch, manage your online reputation, and cultivate relationships that elevate your brand to new heights. Drawing from examples like Rachel Ford, an entrepreneur who leveraged her personal story to create a thriving business, we'll explore how sharing your journey authentically can inspire others and attract new opportunities.

Whether you're just starting out or refining an existing brand, this chapter offers practical insights to help you build a personal brand that opens doors. As Danish Chandra, a brand strategist, notes, "Consistency breeds trust, and trust builds loyalty." By maintaining a clear and consistent brand, you can stand out in a crowded marketplace and position yourself as an authority in your field.

By the end of this chapter, you'll understand how to harness the power of personal branding to build meaningful connections and establish yourself as a leader. A strong personal brand not only attracts opportunities—it inspires others and becomes the foundation for your legacy. With the tools and insights provided in this chapter, you'll be empowered to become the architect of your own success story, creating a brand that reflects who you are and what you aspire to achieve.

Shonda Rhimes' Success Story: A Trailblazer in Television and Storytelling

"Understanding copyright is not just about protecting your work; it's about empowering it. Knowledge of the law turns your creativity into a sustainable business." — SHONDA RHIMES, TELEVISION PRODUCER AND WRITER

Shonda Rhimes is a prolific writer, producer, and showrunner whose groundbreaking work has transformed television. Best known for creating hit series like Grey's Anatomy, Scandal, and How to Get Away with Murder, Rhimes has become a cultural icon, redefining what it means to tell bold, diverse stories. Her journey from aspiring writer to one of the most influential figures in television history is a testament to her creativity, determination, and fearlessness.

Early Life: A Love for Stories and Creativity
Born on January 13, 1970, in Chicago, Illinois, Shonda Rhimes grew up in a supportive family that encouraged creativity. As the youngest of six children, she was drawn to storytelling from a young age, often inventing elaborate stories for

herself and her siblings. Her passion for film and television grew throughout high school and college.

Rhimes attended Dartmouth College, where she majored in English and pursued her love for writing by participating in theater productions and penning short stories. After graduation, she enrolled in the prestigious MFA program at the USC School of Cinematic Arts, where she honed her skills in screenwriting. Her thesis project won recognition, giving her a taste of the possibilities in Hollywood.

Early Struggles: Breaking into Hollywood

Like many aspiring writers, Rhimes initially found it challenging to break into the entertainment industry. After completing her MFA, she worked on a variety of odd jobs, including directing a documentary about the lives of African American women during the war, titled Hank Aaron: Chasing the Dream. She also worked as a research assistant for the 1995 film *Bridges of Madison County*.

Her big break came when she co-wrote the screenplay for Introducing Dorothy Dandridge (1999), an HBO film starring Halle Berry. The film received critical acclaim, establishing Rhimes as a talented screenwriter. However, major success still eluded her, and she continued to write scripts that were optioned but never produced.

Creating Grey's Anatomy: A Defining Moment

Everything changed for Rhimes in 2005 when she created Grey's Anatomy, a medical drama that would become one of the longest-running shows in television history. Rhimes' idea was to tell a story about ambitious medical interns navigating the challenges of both their professional and personal lives. Her ability to blend drama, romance, and complex characters immediately captivated audiences.

Grey's Anatomy broke new ground for its diverse cast and innovative storytelling, featuring characters from different racial and cultural backgrounds. Rhimes was intentional about defying stereotypes, giving audiences fully developed characters and tackling challenging social issues. The show became an instant hit and set the tone for much of her future work.

Building Shondaland: A Media Empire

With the success of *Grey's Anatomy*, Rhimes founded Shondaland, her own production company. Shondaland went on to produce a series of critically acclaimed and commercially successful shows, including Scandal (2012) and How to Get Away with Murder (2014). Each show featured strong, complicated female leads—like Olivia Pope, played by Kerry Washington, and Annalise Keating, played by Viola Davis—paving the way for greater representation of women and people of color in television.

Rhimes' shows became known for their fast-paced storytelling, intricate plots, and emotional depth. She pushed boundaries, addressing political issues, social justice, and human rights within her narratives. Her work not only entertained but also challenged societal norms, making her a cultural force in television.

The Netflix Deal: A New Era

In 2017, Rhimes made headlines by signing a landmark deal with Netflix, leaving network television behind to create exclusive content for the streaming giant. The multi-year deal was a game-changer for the entertainment industry, reflecting the shift toward streaming platforms as the future of television.

Under the Netflix deal, Rhimes produced the hit series Bridgerton (2020), which became one of the platform's most-watched shows. Known for its bold storytelling and inclusive casting, *Bridgerton* cemented Rhimes' ability to create genre-defying entertainment.

Challenges and Triumphs: Balancing Creativity and Pressure

Rhimes has been open about the challenges of balancing creativity with the pressures of success. Running multiple hit shows at once meant working tirelessly behind the scenes, often facing the demands of managing large productions and maintaining high creative standards.

Despite these challenges, Rhimes remained committed to telling bold stories that reflect the diversity and complexity of real life. She also became a mentor and advocate for underrepresented voices in the entertainment industry, helping pave the way for a more inclusive future.

Legacy and Influence: Redefining Television

Shonda Rhimes' impact on television is profound. She redefined network TV by showcasing complex characters and diverse stories that had rarely been seen before. Rhimes is not just a successful producer—she is a cultural pioneer who has changed the way the industry approaches race, gender, and storytelling.

Her influence extends beyond television. In 2021, she published her memoir, "Year of Yes," a candid account of how she transformed her life by embracing opportunities outside of her comfort zone. The book became a bestseller, inspiring readers to confront their fears and pursue their passions.

Conclusion: A Legacy of Bold Storytelling

Shonda Rhimes' journey from a young storyteller in Chicago to a powerhouse showrunner and media mogul is a story of passion, perseverance, and fearless creativity. Her ability to push boundaries, amplify underrepresented voices, and tell stories that resonate globally has earned her a lasting legacy as one of the most influential figures in television history.

Through Shondaland, Rhimes continues to shape the future of entertainment, proving that great stories have the power to change culture and that representation matters.

David Meerman Scott's Success Story: The Pioneer of Modern Marketing and Real-Time Strategies

"Mastering media magic means transforming limited resources into limitless potential, proving that with creativity and strategy, even the smallest PR budget can produce a blockbuster impact." — DAVID MEERMAN SCOTT, MARKETING STRATEGIST

David Meerman Scott is a marketing strategist, keynote speaker, and bestselling author known for transforming the way businesses engage with customers in the digital age. His groundbreaking insights into real-time marketing, content creation, and social media have helped businesses around the world embrace new marketing paradigms. Scott's career reflects a passion for breaking traditional rules and empowering companies to connect directly with their audiences.

Early Life: A Curious Mind for Business and Communication

David Meerman Scott was born on March 25, 1961, in the United States. His early life was shaped by a love for travel, exploration, and storytelling. After earning a degree in economics from Kenyon College, he pursued a career in financial journalism, working in Asia for several years. His experience in international finance exposed him to the importance of timely information and the challenges businesses face when navigating global markets.

After returning to the U.S., Scott transitioned to a career in corporate marketing. He worked for companies such as NewsEdge Corporation, where he managed marketing efforts focused on delivering real-time news services to businesses. His time in the corporate world gave him insight into outdated marketing strategies and fueled his interest in how the internet could revolutionize communication.

A Turning Point: Embracing the Power of the Internet

In the early 2000s, Scott recognized that the traditional marketing funnel—built around advertising, press releases, and outbound sales—was becoming obsolete. The rise of the internet and social media allowed businesses to engage directly with consumers, bypassing gatekeepers like journalists and advertising agencies. This realization became the foundation of his marketing philosophy.

Scott left the corporate world to pursue a career as a consultant and thought leader, determined to help businesses adapt to the digital landscape. In 2007, he published "The New Rules of Marketing & PR," a groundbreaking book that outlined how organizations could leverage blogs, social media, and real-time communication to build relationships with customers. The book became an instant bestseller and has since been translated into over 30 languages.

The New Rules of Marketing & PR: A Game-Changer

Scott's book, *The New Rules of Marketing & PR*, redefined the way companies approach marketing, public relations, and communication. He argued that businesses needed to move away from interruptive advertising and instead focus on creating valuable content that resonates with their audience. His message emphasized the importance of:

- Creating content that solves problems and adds value to customers' lives.

- Engaging with audiences in real time through social media and blogs.

- Building direct relationships with consumers, rather than relying on traditional advertising and media channels.

The book became a standard in marketing education, widely adopted by universities and businesses. It is now in its seventh edition, reflecting the ever-changing landscape of digital marketing.

Speaking and Consulting: Spreading the Message Worldwide

As the success of his book grew, Scott became a sought-after keynote speaker, delivering talks at conferences and events worldwide. His dynamic presentations focus on real-time marketing strategies and how businesses can stay ahead of trends by acting quickly and authentically. Scott's ability to engage audiences and simplify complex marketing concepts has earned him a place among the top marketing thought leaders.

In addition to his public speaking, Scott has consulted with companies of all sizes, from startups to global enterprises. His approach emphasizes empowering businesses to think independently and adopt a customer-centric mindset, encouraging them to create authentic connections with their audiences.

Expanding Influence: The Power of Fanocracy

In 2020, Scott co-authored "Fanocracy: Turning Fans into Customers and Customers into Fans" with his daughter, Reiko Scott. The book explores how businesses can build loyal communities by treating customers like fans and creating emotional connections with them. Scott draws examples from the world of sports, entertainment, and business, demonstrating how fan culture can foster brand loyalty and drive success.

Fanocracy became another bestseller, resonating with businesses looking to create meaningful, lasting relationships with their customers. It reflects Scott's belief that in the modern world, connection and authenticity are more important than ever.

Legacy and Impact: A Visionary for the Digital Age

David Meerman Scott's influence on digital marketing and communication is profound. His ideas have redefined marketing strategies for countless businesses, encouraging them to embrace real-time interaction and authentic storytelling. His emphasis on providing value through content has become a foundational principle of inbound marketing.

Today, Scott continues to inspire entrepreneurs, marketers, and business leaders through his books, speeches, and consulting. He remains an advocate for innovation and creativity, urging businesses to challenge outdated practices and stay ahead in an ever-evolving digital world.

Conclusion: A Legacy of Real-Time Connection

David Meerman Scott's journey from journalist to marketing thought leader is a story of curiosity, adaptability, and passion for innovation. His ability to identify emerging trends and help businesses navigate the digital landscape has cemented his reputation as a pioneer in marketing and communication. Through his books, speeches, and consulting work, Scott continues to empower businesses to connect authentically with customers and thrive in the modern world. His impact on marketing strategy and real-time communication will undoubtedly shape the industry for years to come.

———

Rebecca Lieb's Success Story: A Pioneer in Content Marketing and Digital Strategy

"Content is the atomic particle of all digital marketing." — REBECCA LIEB, DIGITAL ADVERTISING AND MEDIA ANALYST

Rebecca Lieb is a digital marketing expert, author, and thought leader who has shaped the evolution of content marketing, digital advertising, and media strategy. As a trusted advisor to some of the world's largest brands and a respected voice in the marketing world, Lieb has pioneered frameworks and strategies that have empowered businesses to succeed in the digital era. Through her books, consulting work, and thought leadership, Lieb continues to influence and educate marketers on how to thrive in the ever-changing digital landscape.

Early Life and Career: Finding a Passion for Media and Marketing
Rebecca Lieb's career began with a deep-rooted love for media, storytelling, and communication. She initially pursued a career in journalism, where she honed her skills in research, analysis, and content creation. Lieb's work as a journalist gave her insights into how stories shape public opinion and engage audiences, laying the foundation for her future career in content marketing.

As the digital landscape began to evolve, Lieb became fascinated by how technology was transforming media and marketing, shifting traditional paradigms and creating new opportunities for audience engagement. She quickly recognized the potential of content as a strategic tool for brands, inspiring her to move from journalism into digital marketing and consulting.

Breaking into Digital Marketing: Shaping a New Discipline
In the early 2000s, Lieb became one of the early adopters of content marketing as a strategic approach to business. She began consulting with brands and publishers, helping them develop effective content strategies to reach and engage their target audiences. Her experience as a journalist gave her a unique perspective on how businesses could create valuable content that resonated with customers without relying solely on advertising.

Lieb was instrumental in defining content marketing at a time when it was still an emerging discipline. Her work emphasized the importance of consistent, high-quality content across digital channels to build trust, drive engagement, and generate long-term value for businesses.

Thought Leadership: Writing the Playbook for Content Strategy
In 2012, Lieb published her influential book, "Content Marketing: Think Like a Publisher," which became a seminal work in the field. The book provided practical advice on how businesses could embrace a publisher mindset, developing editorial calendars, curating content, and measuring results. It introduced frameworks that enabled companies to align content efforts with business goals, and it became an essential guide for marketers, entrepreneurs, and business leaders.

Following the success of her first book, Lieb continued to produce research and thought leadership on topics like native advertising, branded content, and digital media ecosystems. Her writings, published in leading industry publications, further solidified her status as a content marketing pioneer.

A Leader in Industry Research and Consulting

Lieb has worked as a consultant and analyst for several prominent organizations, including Altimeter Group, where she conducted research on content strategy and media trends. She has advised some of the world's leading brands and organizations, helping them develop future-proof marketing strategies and navigate the complexities of digital transformation.

Her consulting work focuses on integrating content into broader marketing strategies, ensuring that businesses deliver the right messages to the right audiences at the right time. Her ability to combine strategic thinking with practical execution has made her a trusted advisor to Fortune 500 companies and marketing teams across industries.

Adapting to Industry Shifts: Staying Ahead of Trends

Lieb's career reflects her ability to anticipate and adapt to industry changes. As marketing technology evolved, she expanded her focus to include topics such as data-driven marketing, artificial intelligence, and voice search, helping brands stay ahead of emerging trends. Her thought leadership on native advertising and branded content played a crucial role in redefining the future of digital advertising, offering alternatives to traditional display ads that engage audiences more effectively.

Lieb continues to explore how new technologies—from AI-powered personalization to content automation—are shaping the future of marketing, ensuring that her work remains relevant and impactful.

Legacy and Influence: Educating the Next Generation

Rebecca Lieb's influence extends beyond consulting and writing—she is also a respected educator and speaker. She regularly delivers keynote presentations at industry events and conferences, sharing insights on content strategy, digital marketing trends, and media innovation. Her ability to simplify complex topics and provide actionable advice has made her a sought-after speaker and educator.

Lieb's legacy lies in her ability to connect the dots between media, content, and technology, providing businesses with the tools they need to thrive in the digital era. Her work has inspired a generation of marketers, content creators, and business leaders to embrace storytelling, adapt to change, and build meaningful connections with their audiences.

Conclusion: A Visionary in Content Marketing and Digital Strategy

Rebecca Lieb's career is a story of innovation, insight, and leadership. From her early days in journalism to becoming a pioneer in content marketing, she has consistently pushed the boundaries of what is possible in digital media and marketing. Through her books, consulting work, and thought leadership, Lieb has transformed how businesses engage with audiences and leverage content as a strategic asset.

As the digital landscape continues to evolve, Rebecca Lieb remains a visionary force, guiding companies through the challenges and opportunities of content marketing and digital strategy. Her legacy is one of empowerment and education, proving that with the right strategy, content can drive both business success and meaningful engagement.

Naomi Simmons' Success Story: Bridging Authors and Readers Through Strategic Publishing

"IngramSpark isn't just a distribution platform; it's a bridge connecting your books to a world of readers across diverse markets, making your literary voice echo globally." — NAOMI SIMMONS, PUBLISHING STRATEGIST

Naomi Simmons is a publishing strategist, author, and expert in self-publishing and distribution, known for helping authors leverage platforms like IngramSpark to reach global audiences. Her quote, *"IngramSpark isn't just a distribution platform; it's a bridge connecting your books to a world of readers across diverse markets, making your literary voice echo globally,"* reflects her belief in the power of strategic distribution to amplify an author's impact. Simmons' career is a testament to the idea that great publishing is not just about writing books—but also about creating pathways for them to thrive.

Early Life and Passion for Education
Naomi Simmons' journey into the publishing world was rooted in a love for education, books, and storytelling. From a young age, she displayed a passion for language learning and creative communication, which would later guide her career. Her early work focused on teaching English as a second language (ESL), where she honed her skills in curriculum design and educational publishing.

Simmons' career began with writing educational content for young learners, creating engaging learning materials for both traditional classrooms and home education. Her ability to combine pedagogy with creativity made her a sought-after expert in children's educational publishing. Over time, Simmons recognized the growing demand for self-publishing platforms, and her career took a natural turn toward guiding authors through the publishing landscape.

Transition to Publishing Strategy: Mastering IngramSpark
As digital publishing and print-on-demand technology became more accessible, Simmons saw an opportunity to help authors take control of their publishing journeys. She became a passionate advocate for self-publishing platforms, focusing on IngramSpark, a powerful tool for authors seeking global reach and market distribution.

Through her consulting work, Simmons helped authors understand how to maximize IngramSpark's distribution capabilities, ensuring their books could reach brick-and-mortar bookstores, libraries, and online retailers worldwide. She developed a step-by-step process to help authors navigate everything from ISBN assignment and metadata optimization to book marketing strategies. Her work emphasized the importance of quality production, helping authors produce professional books that compete on the global stage.

Building a Reputation as a Publishing Strategist
Simmons became known for her strategic insights and practical advice in the self-publishing community. Her approach is rooted in empowerment—teaching authors how to build sustainable careers by understanding the business side of publishing. Whether through one-on-one coaching, webinars, or public speaking

engagements, Simmons offers actionable advice that helps authors bring their books to market effectively.

She also contributed to educational resources for independent authors, writing guides and hosting workshops on distribution channels, pricing strategies, and marketing plans. Her reputation as a publishing strategist grew, attracting collaborations with authors across genres—from fiction and nonfiction to children's books and academic works.

Overcoming Challenges: Navigating a Changing Industry

Simmons' work reflects her ability to adapt to the ever-changing publishing landscape. As more authors entered the self-publishing space, Simmons helped them navigate common challenges, such as discoverability in a crowded market and standing out among competitors. She emphasized that success in publishing requires more than just great content—it also demands strong marketing, professional presentation, and strategic distribution.

During times of uncertainty, like the COVID-19 pandemic, Simmons worked tirelessly to help authors adjust to shifting consumer behavior and digital-first strategies. She taught authors to leverage online platforms creatively, ensuring their books reached readers when physical bookstores were less accessible.

Legacy and Impact in the Publishing World

Today, Naomi Simmons is recognized as a leading voice in self-publishing and distribution strategy, inspiring authors to embrace the opportunities that modern platforms like IngramSpark offer. Her philosophy emphasizes empowerment through knowledge, helping authors understand that publishing is both an art and a business. Simmons' guidance has enabled countless writers to share their stories with the world and build sustainable careers as independent authors.

Her influence extends beyond individual projects—through her work, Simmons has helped shape the self-publishing ecosystem, encouraging platforms like IngramSpark to evolve in response to author needs. Her practical approach to publishing strategy and distribution continues to inspire new generations of writers to embrace the global potential of their literary works.

Conclusion: Connecting Voices with Readers Worldwide

Naomi Simmons' journey from educational content creator to publishing strategist highlights the importance of strategic thinking in the publishing world. Her ability to bridge the gap between authors and readers through IngramSpark and other distribution platforms has made her a trusted guide in the self-publishing community.

Her story is one of innovation, empowerment, and perseverance, proving that with the right strategy, authors can reach readers across the globe and turn their literary dreams into reality. Through her work, Simmons has built a legacy that echoes beyond bookshelves, helping authors unlock their potential and connect with audiences worldwide.

Lisa Scottoline's Success Story: From Lawyer to Bestselling Author

"Building a successful writing team is like orchestrating a symphony; each member plays a unique part, but together they create a harmonious masterpiece that resonates beyond the pages." — LISA SCOTTOLINE, BESTSELLING AUTHOR

Lisa Scottoline is a renowned American author known for her legal thrillers, emotional family dramas, and crime novels. With over 30 million copies of her books in print, Scottoline has earned a place among the most successful writers of her genre. Her journey from a lawyer to a bestselling novelist is a story of resilience, creativity, and a relentless pursuit of her passion for storytelling.

Early Life: A Passion for Literature and Law

Lisa Scottoline was born on July 1, 1955, in Philadelphia, Pennsylvania. From a young age, she displayed a love for reading and writing, immersing herself in stories of mystery, law, and justice. She pursued her passion for learning at the University of Pennsylvania, where she earned a degree in English.

Although her heart belonged to writing, Scottoline also felt drawn to the legal world. She enrolled in the University of Pennsylvania Law School, where she graduated with honors and began working as a litigation attorney at a prestigious law firm in Philadelphia.

The Turning Point: A Leap into Writing
After practicing law for several years, Scottoline decided to step away from her legal career to raise her daughter as a single mother. During this time, she rekindled her passion for writing. Inspired by her background in law, she began working on her first novel, determined to combine her legal knowledge with her love for storytelling.

However, the road to publication wasn't easy. Scottoline's early efforts to get published were met with rejection, but she remained persistent. Her belief in her stories and her determination to succeed as an author kept her going.

Breakthrough with Legal Thrillers
In 1994, Scottoline published her debut novel, "Everywhere That Mary Went," introducing readers to a new kind of legal thriller that blended suspense with humor and emotional depth. The novel, which followed the adventures of a female lawyer navigating both professional challenges and personal conflicts, resonated with readers. It was nominated for the Edgar Award for Best First Novel, marking the beginning of Scottoline's career as a novelist.

Following the success of her first book, Scottoline continued writing legal thrillers featuring strong female protagonists. Her novels often delve into complex legal cases, but they also explore family dynamics, friendship, and personal growth, offering a fresh take on the traditional legal thriller genre.

A Bestselling Career and Critical Acclaim
Scottoline's ability to craft engaging characters and gripping plots quickly earned her a loyal readership. Her novels, including titles like "Mistaken Identity," "Think Twice," and "Betrayed," became bestsellers, cementing her reputation as one of the leading voices in legal thrillers. She won several awards throughout her career, including the prestigious Edgar Award.

Beyond legal thrillers, Scottoline began writing family dramas and memoir-style essays, demonstrating her versatility as an author. Her novels, such as "Eternal" (2021), reflect a deeper exploration of historical fiction, broadening her literary scope. These books resonate with readers not only for their thrilling plots but also for their emotional resonance and humor.

Challenges and Triumphs: Balancing Life and Writing

As a single mother raising her daughter while pursuing a writing career, Scottoline's journey wasn't without challenges. However, her ability to balance personal and professional life became one of the defining themes of her work. Her writing often explores the complexities of family relationships and the strength of women overcoming obstacles—mirroring her own experiences.

Scottoline also collaborated with her daughter, Francesca Serritella, on a series of humorous essay collections that reflect on their mother-daughter relationship. These collections, such as "Why My Third Husband Will Be a Dog," highlight her gift for humor and her ability to connect with readers on a personal level.

Legacy and Influence

Lisa Scottoline's influence extends beyond her bestselling books. She has become a mentor and advocate for aspiring writers, regularly speaking at conferences, workshops, and book events. Her engaging personality and approachable writing style have earned her a loyal following among readers and writers alike.

In addition to her literary achievements, Scottoline is known for her charitable efforts and involvement in the Philadelphia community. She remains committed to giving back, supporting causes related to literacy, education, and women's empowerment.

Conclusion: A Legacy of Legal Thrills and Heartfelt Stories

Lisa Scottoline's journey from a litigation attorney to a bestselling author is a story of persistence, creativity, and reinvention. Through her legal thrillers, family dramas, and humorous essays, she has captured the hearts of readers worldwide. Her ability to weave together suspense, emotion, and humor has made her one of the most versatile and beloved authors of our time.

Today, Scottoline continues to write, inspire, and connect with her audience, proving that stories have the power to entertain, heal, and transform lives. Her legacy is one of resilience, creativity, and passion, leaving an indelible mark on the world of literature.

Rachel Ford's Success Story: Navigating Publishing Success through Strategic Alignment

"Getting published under an Amazon imprint isn't just about writing a great book; it's about strategically aligning your manuscript to meet the discerning eyes of specific imprints, each with its own unique flavor and audience." — RACHEL FORD,
PUBLISHING STRATEGIST

Rachel Ford is a publishing strategist and author with deep expertise in leveraging Amazon imprints to help writers align their work with the right audience and publishing channels. Known for her insight that *"Getting published under an Amazon imprint isn't just about writing a great book; it's about strategically aligning your manuscript to meet the discerning eyes of specific imprints, each with its own unique flavor and audience,"* Ford has made a name for herself by guiding authors through the intricacies of the Amazon publishing ecosystem.

Early Life: A Dual Passion for Technology and Storytelling
Rachel Ford's background reflects a blend of technology and creativity. As a software engineer by day and an author by night, Ford brings a unique perspective to the publishing industry. Her love for storytelling and problem-solving led her to publish over 60 books in genres such as science fiction, paranormal mystery, and thrillers, while her technical background sharpened her skills in research, marketing, and digital strategy.

This combination of skills provided Ford with a unique insight into self-publishing platforms like Amazon KDP, which rely heavily on metadata, keywords, and algorithms to maximize book visibility. Her experience enabled her to develop strategies that help authors navigate these complexities and position their books to align with the expectations of different imprints and audiences.

Mastering Amazon Imprints: A Strategic Approach
Ford's expertise lies in helping authors strategically position their manuscripts to align with the criteria and preferences of various Amazon imprints, such as Thomas & Mercer (for thrillers), Montlake (for romance), and 47North (for speculative fiction). She emphasizes that while writing a great book is crucial,

understanding the subtle differences between imprints—including the types of stories and narrative voices they favor—is just as important.

Through her consulting work and workshops, Ford teaches authors how to:

- Research and identify the most suitable imprint for their genre and writing style.

- Refine manuscripts to meet specific market expectations.

- Optimize their book proposals with strategic keywords, metadata, and pitch elements.

Her approach ensures that authors are not just submitting great books but are also targeting the right audience with precision, increasing their chances of securing publishing deals under the right Amazon imprint.

Challenges and Growth in a Competitive Industry

The path to success in Amazon publishing is not without its challenges. With the rapidly evolving market and fierce competition among self-published authors, Ford's strategies help her clients stand out. She emphasizes the importance of continuous learning and adaptation, encouraging writers to stay updated on trends in reader behavior and industry standards.

Ford also advocates for building author platforms through social media, newsletters, and personal branding, reinforcing the idea that visibility and engagement are crucial for long-term success in self-publishing.

Legacy and Impact: Empowering Authors to Thrive

Today, Rachel Ford is recognized as a thought leader in the self-publishing world. Her work not only helps authors get their books into the hands of readers but also demystifies the complex process of publishing under major imprints. Through her consulting services, online courses, and speaking engagements, Ford has inspired a new generation of independent authors to take control of their publishing journeys.

Her story exemplifies how strategic thinking and alignment with market opportunities can transform a manuscript into a published success. As the publishing world continues to evolve, Ford remains at the forefront, guiding authors through the challenges and opportunities of modern self-publishing.

Conclusion: Building Bridges between Authors and Audiences

Rachel Ford's career reflects the art and science of publishing, demonstrating that success in the digital age requires more than just creative talent—it demands strategic alignment with the right channels and audiences. By helping authors navigate Amazon imprints and self-publishing platforms, Ford continues to connect literary voices with readers across the globe, leaving a lasting impact on the independent publishing landscape.

Max Harmon's Success Story: Mastering the Art of Immersive Audio

"Great audio doesn't just tell a story; it immerses you in it. With the right soundscape, listeners can hear the whisper of the wind and feel the tension in a silence, turning passive listening into an active adventure." — MAX HARMON, AUDIO ENGINEER

Max Harmon is an audio engineer and sound designer known for his ability to transform audio into an immersive experience, creating soundscapes that transport listeners into the heart of a story. His quote, *"Great audio doesn't just tell a story; it immerses you in it. With the right soundscape, listeners can hear the whisper of the wind and feel the tension in a silence, turning passive listening into an active adventure,"* reflects his philosophy: sound is not merely heard—it is felt. Harmon's journey to becoming a sought-after audio expert is a story of technical expertise, creative artistry, and a relentless pursuit of excellence in the field of sound engineering.

Early Life: A Passion for Sound

From an early age, Harmon was fascinated by sound and technology. Growing up, he spent countless hours experimenting with musical instruments, recording devices, and audio equipment, developing an ear for subtle audio elements that often go unnoticed. His love for both music and storytelling drove him to explore how sound shapes human experience, from the ambiance in films to the richness of a live performance.

Harmon pursued a degree in audio engineering and sound design, where he learned the technical aspects of sound production, including mixing, mastering, and acoustics. His time in university helped him develop the technical proficiency needed to manipulate sound while nurturing his creative vision for audio storytelling.

Breaking into the Industry: Early Work and Breakthroughs

After graduation, Harmon began his career working in recording studios, collaborating with musicians to produce albums and soundtracks. His ability to blend creativity with technical precision soon earned him a reputation for crafting clean, dynamic audio tracks. In addition to studio work, Harmon branched out into sound design for podcasts, audiobooks, and film, experimenting with immersive soundscapes that engaged listeners on a deeper level.

His breakthrough came when he worked on a highly acclaimed podcast series, where his sound effects and ambient elements elevated the storytelling, making listeners feel like they were part of the narrative. This project demonstrated Harmon's philosophy that great audio transforms passive listening into an active, emotional experience.

Crafting Immersive Soundscapes: Harmon's Philosophy and Process

Harmon's approach to audio design is rooted in his belief that every sound matters. Whether it's the faint hum of an engine or the silence between conversations, Harmon understands that each element contributes to the overall experience. He focuses on creating rich, layered soundscapes that draw the listener in, using techniques such as:

- Field recordings to capture authentic environmental sounds.

- 3D audio techniques to create spatial sound effects that mimic real-world acoustics.

- Dynamic mixing to emphasize moments of tension, emotion, or stillness in the narrative.

Harmon also works closely with producers and directors to ensure that the audio aligns perfectly with the story's vision, creating a seamless blend of dialogue, music, and effects that enhances the emotional impact.

Success and Influence in the Audio Industry

Max Harmon's work spans across film, podcasting, video games, and live performances, and he has become a go-to sound designer for projects that require immersive, high-quality audio. His ability to elevate stories through sound has earned him collaborations with top-tier production companies and independent creators alike.

Harmon's success lies not only in his technical mastery but also in his creative intuition. His soundscapes tell stories, evoke emotions, and transport listeners into other worlds, setting new standards for immersive audio experiences.

Adapting to Industry Trends: Embracing New Technologies

As the audio industry evolves, Harmon remains at the forefront by adopting emerging technologies. He is a pioneer in spatial audio and 3D sound, exploring how these technologies can create even more immersive experiences for virtual reality (VR) and augmented reality (AR) projects. His curiosity and drive to push the boundaries of sound design keep him ahead of the curve in an industry that is constantly evolving.

Harmon is also an advocate for accessibility in audio, ensuring that his projects are inclusive by incorporating features like audio descriptions and making soundscapes accessible to people with diverse auditory needs.

Legacy and Continued Innovation

Max Harmon's influence extends beyond individual projects—he is committed to mentoring aspiring audio engineers and sharing his knowledge through workshops and speaking engagements. His passion for collaborating with creators from different fields—from filmmakers to podcasters—has fostered a community where audio professionals can learn, experiment, and grow together.

Conclusion: A Legacy in Sound

Max Harmon's career is a testament to the power of sound to shape stories and evoke emotions. Through his mastery of audio engineering and sound design, Harmon has transformed the way audiences experience sound, creating immersive adventures that transcend traditional listening. His journey from early experimentation with sound to becoming a renowned audio expert exemplifies the magic that happens when technical skill meets creative passion.

In an industry where the right soundscape can turn a good project into a masterpiece, Max Harmon's work continues to inspire and elevate, proving that great audio is not just heard—it is experienced.

———————

Manish Chandra's Success Story: The Visionary Behind Poshmark's Social Shopping Revolution

"Building a successful business is about more than just transactions; it's about creating meaningful connections. At Poshmark, we've built a community where every closet tells a story, and every sale strengthens that connection. When you focus on empowering people, the business will grow naturally." — MANISH CHANDRA, VISIONARY LEADER IN SOCIAL COMMERCE

Poshmark (often mistakenly referred to as "Posh Mart") is a highly successful online marketplace that specializes in fashion, allowing users to buy and sell new or second-hand clothing and accessories. Its story is one of innovation, timing, and community-building, making it one of the most popular platforms in the social commerce space.

The Founding of Poshmark

Poshmark was founded in 2011 by Manish Chandra, along with co-founders Tracy Sun, Gautam Golwala, and Chetan Pungaliya. The inspiration for the platform came from Chandra's desire to blend social media and e-commerce in a way that would enable users to shop their friends' closets, while also building a community around fashion.

Before Poshmark, Chandra had already ventured into the tech world. He previously founded Kaboodle, a social shopping site that focused on product discovery, which was acquired by Hearst Corporation in 2007. His experience with Kaboodle laid the foundation for his vision of creating a more personalized, community-driven shopping platform with Poshmark.

The Early Days: Social Commerce and Mobile-First
At the time of Poshmark's launch, the resale market was gaining momentum, with platforms like eBay and Craigslist already in play. However, Poshmark differentiated itself by focusing on a mobile-first experience. Chandra believed that shopping should be as easy as sharing a photo, so he developed an app that made it simple for users to snap a picture of their item, upload it, and start selling.

The key innovation that set Poshmark apart was its focus on social interactions. Users could follow each other, like listings, comment on products, and even attend virtual "Posh Parties"—real-time, themed shopping events where users could list and buy items. This combination of social media dynamics with e-commerce made the platform highly engaging, creating a sense of community that was critical to its early success.

Growth and Expansion
Poshmark's mobile-first strategy paid off as smartphone use grew rapidly during the early 2010s. The ease of listing products through a phone and the sense of community attracted a growing base of millennial and Gen Z users who were looking for sustainable fashion options or who wanted to build their own resale businesses.

As the platform grew, Poshmark expanded beyond women's fashion into men's fashion, kids' clothing, accessories, and even home goods. The company's ability to adapt to market demands and diversify its offerings helped fuel its growth.

By focusing on empowering individual sellers, many of whom were women and part-time entrepreneurs, Poshmark quickly became a destination for side hustlers and micro-entrepreneurs. The simplicity of the app, combined with the community-building features, made it an ideal platform for people to sell both luxury and everyday items, whether they were cleaning out their closet or building a business.

Going Public and Continued Success
In January 2021, Poshmark went public on the NASDAQ stock exchange under the ticker symbol POSH. The company's IPO was a success, raising hundreds of millions of dollars and marking a major milestone in the platform's journey from a startup to a publicly traded company.

As of 2024, Poshmark has more than 80 million users across the United States, Canada, Australia, and India, and it has facilitated the sale of millions of items. The platform's success continues to be driven by its ability to adapt to trends, its mobile-first approach, and its commitment to building a community-focused marketplace where users feel empowered to sell and shop sustainably.

Key Factors in Poshmark's Success

1. **Social Commerce Focus**: Poshmark revolutionized resale by combining the interactivity of social media with the convenience of e-commerce. Its community-centric features keep users engaged and foster loyalty.

2. **Mobile-First Approach**: Poshmark's user-friendly app allows people to easily list, browse, and buy items on their phones, aligning perfectly with the growing trend of mobile shopping.

3. **Empowering Sellers**: The platform has provided opportunities for individual sellers to monetize their closets or build small businesses. The "Posher" community has become an essential part of the company's identity.

4. **Sustainability**: As the fashion industry becomes increasingly aware of its environmental impact, Poshmark's model of encouraging second-hand shopping has attracted consumers looking for sustainable alternatives to fast fashion.

5. **Innovative Features**: With elements like Posh Parties, bundling options, and social selling tools, Poshmark has remained ahead of the curve in terms of user engagement and creating a vibrant, interactive marketplace.

Conclusion: A Fashion Powerhouse

Poshmark's story is a testament to the power of blending technology, commerce, and community. What began as a small, mobile-driven resale platform has grown into a multibillion-dollar global marketplace for fashion and lifestyle items. Through continuous innovation, a focus on sustainability, and empowering individuals to become entrepreneurs, Poshmark has carved out a unique and successful niche in the world of e-commerce.

CHAPTER FIVE

Mastering Efficiency and Time Leadership

Time is the most precious resource for any entrepreneur or business leader, and mastering time management is essential for achieving both personal and professional success. Unlike money or material assets, time cannot be replenished once it's spent. In today's fast-paced, constantly connected world, the ability to manage time effectively is what separates high achievers from those who struggle to meet their goals. Clay Clark, business coach and entrepreneur, emphasizes: "Time isn't just a resource—it's the key to unlocking your future." This chapter delves into how practical time management strategies can unlock your potential, helping you take control of your schedule and lead more efficiently.

Effective time management goes beyond filling calendars or checking off to-do lists—it requires aligning your daily activities with your most significant goals. Doris Fleischer, productivity expert, reminds us: "Success is the result of knowing what's important and doing it consistently." In this chapter, we'll explore how setting clear priorities ensures that time is invested in the things that matter most—

whether that's growing your business, maintaining relationships, or focusing on your well-being. You'll learn how to break large goals into manageable tasks that fit seamlessly into your daily routine.

The concept of balance is also vital to productivity. Liana Evans, digital marketing strategist, advises: "Balance isn't a destination—it's a process you create every day." We'll explore practical ways to achieve balance by scheduling with intention, ensuring that work, personal life, and well-being coexist harmoniously. Structured routines with built-in flexibility enable you to manage unexpected challenges without feeling overwhelmed.

Managing distractions is another critical aspect of effective time leadership. In an age where constant notifications pull us in multiple directions, Tim Wu, the scholar behind "net neutrality," emphasizes the need for focus: "To lead efficiently, you must protect your attention like it's your greatest asset." We'll guide you through strategies like time-blocking, creating environments conducive to deep work, and eliminating unnecessary distractions. Additionally, we'll highlight how intentional breaks can boost productivity rather than hinder it.

Delegation is an essential skill in time management, allowing leaders to focus on high-impact activities. Jim Barksdale, former CEO of Netscape, notes: "Great leaders know what to do—and what to delegate." This chapter will show you how to identify tasks that can be outsourced or assigned to others, empowering your team while freeing you to focus on critical initiatives. Whether you're leading a team or working independently, mastering delegation helps prevent burnout and ensures sustainable growth.

Technology plays a crucial role in streamlining processes and boosting productivity. Lawrence Lessig, legal scholar and innovator, highlights: "The right tools don't just save time—they transform how you work." We'll introduce you to project management software, automation tools, and productivity hacks that help you optimize workflows, reducing time spent on administrative tasks so you can focus on strategic priorities.

Effective time management isn't about packing more activities into your day— it's about making deliberate choices. Leah Turner, performance coach, advises: "Efficiency isn't doing more; it's doing the right things with precision." This chapter encourages you to adopt a quality-over-quantity mindset, focusing on the few activities that truly move the needle and executing them with excellence.

Finally, we'll explore real-world examples of individuals and businesses that mastered time management to achieve remarkable success. Their stories demonstrate that even the most accomplished professionals face time-management challenges, but with the right strategies, they maintain productivity and a healthy work-life balance.

By the end of this chapter, you'll have a toolkit of strategies to improve your time management and productivity. Whether you're striving to hit tight deadlines, scale your business, or reclaim personal time, the principles outlined here will help you maximize each day. As Clay Clark reminds us: "Time is the one resource you control completely—how you use it defines your success." With disciplined time management, you'll create habits that fuel long-term success and unlock your full potential.

———————

Clay Clark's Success Story: Entrepreneur and Business Coach Extraordinaire

"Show me the laws, and I'll show you how to craft content that dazzles while staying within the lines." — CLAY CLARK, ENTREPRENEUR AND BUSINESS COACH

Clay Clark is a serial entrepreneur, business coach, author, and podcast host, known for his ability to help businesses grow through strategic systems and practical mentorship. Throughout his career, Clark has founded multiple successful companies and developed a reputation as a dynamic leader in business education. His signature coaching platform, the ThriveTime Show, has earned him recognition as a leading voice in business coaching by topping the iTunes business podcast charts multiple times.

Early Life: Building a Business from the Ground Up

Clark's entrepreneurial journey began early in life. While still in college, he founded DJConnection.com, a DJ entertainment company that grew into one of the largest wedding entertainment providers in the region. Clark's experience running DJConnection taught him the importance of systems, delegation, and scaling operations—insights that would later become the foundation for his business coaching career.

After selling DJConnection.com, Clark launched several more ventures, including Epic Photos, EITRLounge, and TipTopK9, each focusing on leveraging strong operational frameworks and strategic marketing to drive growth. His businesses ranged from wedding photography to pet training services, showcasing his versatility as an entrepreneur.

ThriveTime Show and Business Coaching: A Mission to Educate Entrepreneurs

In 2016, Clay Clark launched the ThriveTime Show, a business coaching platform and podcast aimed at providing real-world advice and mentorship for entrepreneurs. Branded as "business school without the BS," the ThriveTime Show offers actionable tips on topics such as sales, marketing, hiring, and personal growth. The platform has attracted thousands of subscribers and helped many small business owners grow their companies.

Clark's ThriveTime Show became a top-rated business podcast on iTunes, earning accolades for its entertaining and informative format. Through workshops, one-on-one coaching, and online content, Clark has mentored business leaders and entrepreneurs from a variety of industries, helping them develop repeatable systems for sustainable success.

Entrepreneurial Philosophy: Systems Over Chaos

Clark's approach to business emphasizes efficiency and systems thinking. He believes that entrepreneurs can achieve more by delegating effectively and focusing on processes that scale. His coaching sessions often cover time management, leadership, and operational efficiency, aiming to equip business owners with the tools to work on their business, not just in it.

A favorite principle Clark emphasizes is that success is the result of persistence and mentorship. He encourages aspiring entrepreneurs to find mentors, apply proven strategies, and overcome fear or hesitation by taking consistent action. His work is deeply focused on helping people break free from limiting beliefs and unlock their potential.

Awards and Recognition

Throughout his career, Clay Clark has received numerous accolades, including being named Oklahoma's U.S. SBA Entrepreneur of the Year. His success stories span industries ranging from entertainment and photography to e-commerce and pet training. Beyond his entrepreneurial ventures, Clark is a respected speaker and consultant, working with major companies such as Hewlett Packard, Maytag, and O'Reilly Auto Parts.

Legacy: Inspiring Entrepreneurs to Thrive

Clark's impact extends far beyond his personal businesses. Through his ThriveTime Show platform and business coaching, he has empowered thousands of entrepreneurs to take control of their businesses and grow sustainably. His message is one of resilience, discipline, and strategic thinking, inspiring countless business owners to find joy in entrepreneurship and build meaningful ventures.

Whether through his business coaching programs or public speaking engagements, Clay Clark continues to mentor the next generation of entrepreneurs, leaving a legacy of inspired leadership and practical wisdom.

Conclusion: Turning Experience into Education

Clay Clark's journey from a college DJ entrepreneur to a successful business coach and mentor highlights the power of systems, strategy, and mentorship. With a passion for helping others succeed, Clark has created thriving businesses and platforms that empower entrepreneurs to achieve sustainable growth. His message resonates with those looking to turn challenges into opportunities, building businesses that not only grow but also create lasting value.

Clark's ThriveTime Show continues to be a beacon of practical business education, proving that any entrepreneur, with the right systems in place, can thrive in today's competitive market.

Doris Fleischer's Success Story: Mastering the Art of Public Relations and Narrative Building

"Leadership in public relations doesn't just manage perception—it creates reality, guiding narratives that resonate deeply and inspire action across audiences." — DORIS FLEISCHER, RENOWNED PR STRATEGIST

Doris Fleischer is a renowned public relations strategist, celebrated for her ability to guide narratives that shape perceptions and inspire meaningful action. Her quote, *"Leadership in public relations doesn't just manage perception—it creates reality, guiding narratives that resonate deeply and inspire action across audiences,"* captures her philosophy on the transformative power of PR.

Fleischer's approach emphasizes that successful PR goes beyond spin, focusing instead on creating authentic stories that connect with diverse audiences. Her career reflects a blend of strategic insight and emotional intelligence, making her a sought-after expert in public communication and narrative design.

Foundations: Blending Strategy with Communication

Fleischer's career began in the early days of public relations, where she quickly developed a reputation for crafting compelling campaigns. She recognized that PR professionals must not only manage perceptions but also craft realities, guiding organizations to align their internal values with public narratives.

Over the years, Fleischer has collaborated with companies, nonprofits, and government agencies, designing strategies that resonate with stakeholders and build trust. Her ability to analyze public sentiment and anticipate trends has allowed her to lead high-impact campaigns across industries.

PR Philosophy: Creating Reality through Narrative

Fleischer's unique perspective focuses on the power of narrative to shape reality. She teaches that leaders in PR must align messaging with action, ensuring that the stories organizations tell reflect their values and goals. This alignment builds trust and credibility with audiences, fostering deeper connections and long-term loyalty.

Her approach also emphasizes proactive communication during crises, advocating for transparency and empathy. Fleischer believes that effective PR is not reactive but anticipatory, creating narratives that guide public perception before issues arise.

Impact and Legacy

Throughout her career, Fleischer has become a mentor and thought leader in the PR industry, helping businesses and professionals develop the skills to tell stories that inspire change. She is known for her ability to bridge organizational strategy with public sentiment, creating campaigns that drive both action and connection.

Her philosophy continues to shape the next generation of public relations professionals, inspiring them to embrace storytelling as a strategic tool. Fleischer's work has left a lasting impact on the field of PR, proving that narratives are not just managed—they are built to inspire.

Tim Wu's Success Story: A Pioneer in Technology Law and Antitrust Advocacy

"As we look ahead, the evolution of copyright will increasingly intersect with technology, requiring adaptive legal frameworks to manage the balance between protecting creators and enabling innovation." — TIM WU, PROFESSOR AT COLUMBIA LAW SCHOOL AND A PROMINENT ADVOCATE FOR ANTITRUST AND INTERNET POLICIES

Tim Wu is a professor at Columbia Law School and a leading advocate for antitrust policies, internet freedom, and intellectual property reform. Known for coining the term "net neutrality," Wu has had a profound impact on technology law and policy, shaping debates about the balance between innovation and regulation. His quote, *"As we look ahead, the evolution of copyright will increasingly intersect with technology, requiring adaptive legal frameworks to manage the balance between protecting creators and enabling innovation,"* reflects his forward-thinking perspective on copyright reform in the digital age.

Early Life and Academic Path

Born in Washington, D.C., Wu earned a bachelor's degree from McGill University before attending Harvard Law School, where he excelled as both a student and editor of the Harvard Law Review. After graduating, he worked as a law clerk for Justice Stephen Breyer of the U.S. Supreme Court, gaining valuable insight into the intersection of law and policy.

Breakthrough: Defining Net Neutrality

Wu's career took off with the publication of "Network Neutrality, Broadband Discrimination" in 2003. His concept of net neutrality argued that internet service providers (ISPs) should treat all data equally, preventing them from favoring or blocking specific content. This idea became the foundation for global debates on internet regulation and influenced major regulatory decisions, such as the FCC's Open Internet Order.

Shaping Technology and Antitrust Policy

Beyond net neutrality, Wu has focused on antitrust enforcement in the tech industry. He advocates for breaking up monopolistic companies and regulating tech giants like Google, Facebook, and Amazon, arguing that their dominance stifles competition and innovation. His book "The Curse of Bigness: Antitrust in the New Gilded Age" delves into the dangers of concentrated corporate power and offers solutions through stronger antitrust enforcement.

Wu's work has also extended to copyright reform, where he calls for adaptable frameworks that protect creators while encouraging innovation. His influence has shaped academic discourse, public policy, and regulatory frameworks in the U.S. and beyond.

Public Service and Policy Leadership

Wu has not only excelled in academia but also served in various public roles. In 2021, he joined the Biden Administration as a special assistant for technology and competition policy, where he focused on strengthening antitrust efforts and curbing the excesses of Big Tech.

Throughout his career, Wu has blended academic rigor with real-world impact, shaping policies that govern internet freedom, competition, and intellectual property. His ability to anticipate future challenges has cemented his place as a thought leader in technology and policy circles.

Legacy and Continuing Impact

Tim Wu's career is marked by his commitment to balancing innovation with regulation, ensuring that technology serves the public good. Through his writing, advocacy, and public service, Wu continues to influence the future of digital policy. His work remains essential as the worlds of technology, copyright, and competition law intersect in increasingly complex ways.

His contributions have left an indelible mark on technology law, inspiring future generations to think critically about the role of regulation in a rapidly evolving digital landscape.

<hr>

Liana Evans' Success Story: A Digital Marketing Trailblazer

"Content doesn't win. Optimized content wins." — LIANA EVANS, AUTHOR AND DIGITAL MARKETING EXPERT

Liana Evans is a digital marketing expert, author, and speaker, renowned for her expertise in search engine optimization (SEO), content marketing, and social media strategies. Her quote, *"Content doesn't win. Optimized content wins,"* reflects her belief in the importance of data-driven content optimization for success in the digital landscape.

Early Career: From Technology to Marketing Strategy

Evans started her career in software development before transitioning to digital marketing, combining her technical background with a passion for communications. Her deep understanding of SEO, analytics, and algorithms gave her a competitive edge as she navigated the evolving world of online marketing.

Through various leadership roles in marketing and consulting, Evans developed strategies that emphasized optimization and measurement, ensuring that digital content resonated with the right audiences while driving tangible results.

Publishing Success and Thought Leadership
In 2010, Evans published "Social Media Marketing: Strategies for Engaging in Facebook, Twitter, & Other Social Media," becoming a leading voice on how businesses can integrate social media with SEO and marketing strategies. Her writing and speaking engagements have empowered companies to develop holistic digital marketing strategies, focusing on content performance rather than just content creation.

Evans is a sought-after consultant and speaker at marketing conferences worldwide, where she shares actionable insights on SEO, analytics, and social engagement.

Legacy and Impact: Optimizing for Success
Liana Evans' work exemplifies how content strategy and data analytics intersect to create impactful digital campaigns. Her philosophy encourages businesses to go beyond simple content creation, focusing on optimization and measurable results. She has inspired countless professionals to embrace performance-driven marketing and continues to influence digital marketing best practices globally.

Evans' ability to adapt and lead in a constantly evolving industry solidifies her place as a trailblazer in digital marketing.

Jim Barksdale's Success Story: Transforming Technology and Leadership

"In advertising, data is your compass and creativity your ship; navigating with both ensures you reach the shores of success with precision and flair."
— JIM BARKSDALE, Former CEO of Netscape

Jim Barksdale is a visionary business leader and technology executive best known for his tenure as CEO of Netscape Communications Corporation, where he played a pivotal role in launching one of the first internet browsers and leading the company through a groundbreaking IPO. His career spans influential positions in telecommunications, logistics, and technology, marking him as a key figure in the development of the modern internet economy.

Early Career: Laying the Foundations of Leadership

Barksdale's journey began at IBM, where he gained vital experience in sales and management. From there, he joined Federal Express (FedEx) in the 1980s, where he became instrumental in building FedEx's real-time package tracking system, an innovation that transformed logistics. His work in operations and strategic management contributed significantly to FedEx's rise as a leader in the shipping industry. His experience at FedEx helped him develop a forward-thinking approach to technology and operations, which would become essential later in his career.

Joining Netscape: A Bold Leader in the Browser Wars

In 1995, Barksdale was appointed CEO of Netscape Communications Corporation. At the time, Netscape was at the forefront of internet innovation, providing one of the first widely-used web browsers. Barksdale's strategic leadership guided the company through its initial public offering (IPO), which became a defining moment in the dot-com era. Netscape's IPO is often credited with igniting the first wave of internet investment, making Barksdale a pivotal figure in Silicon Valley's rise.

During his tenure, Barksdale navigated the browser wars—a fierce competition between Netscape and Microsoft. While Microsoft's dominance with Internet Explorer eventually pushed Netscape out of the market, Barksdale's leadership was marked by innovative business strategies and pioneering new internet technologies. Netscape's browser technology laid the groundwork for open web standards that are still in use today.

The AOL Acquisition and Shifting to Philanthropy

In 1999, Netscape was acquired by AOL, marking the end of a significant chapter in Barksdale's career. After the acquisition, he shifted his focus toward philanthropy and public service, using his expertise to contribute to public policy and education initiatives. He served as a member of the President's Foreign Intelligence Advisory Board and participated in advisory roles for the Federal Communications Commission (FCC), where his insight helped shape telecommunications policy.

Barksdale also established the Barksdale Foundation with a focus on improving education and literacy in his home state of Mississippi. The foundation has played a significant role in early childhood education and supports initiatives aimed at boosting literacy rates in underserved communities.

Legacy: Innovator, Leader, and Philanthropist

Jim Barksdale's career embodies a blend of business acumen, technological foresight, and civic responsibility. His time at Netscape not only pioneered early internet technologies but also showcased the importance of resilience and adaptability in the face of fierce competition. His post-corporate career reflects his commitment to giving back, with an emphasis on education and public service.

Barksdale's contributions continue to influence technology, business leadership, and social impact initiatives today. He remains a prominent figure in both the corporate and philanthropic sectors, inspiring future leaders to embrace innovation while focusing on long-term impact. His story exemplifies how visionary leadership and community engagement can shape industries and transform lives.

Lawrence Lessig's Success Story: A Champion of Digital Freedom and Legal Reform

"Fair use is not just a legal defense—it's a vital part of how we innovate and create. Understanding it is essential for anyone who wants to engage with and build upon the cultural dialogue." — LAWRENCE LESSIG, PROFESSOR AND CO-FOUNDER OF CREATIVE COMMONS

"Staying future forward in copyright law means continuously adapting to emerging trends and technological advancements to protect intellectual creativity in the digital age." — LAWRENCE LESSIG, PROFESSOR OF LAW AND LEADERSHIP AT HARVARD LAW SCHOOL AND A LEADING ADVOCATE OF COPYRIGHT REFORM

Lawrence Lessig is a law professor, activist, and advocate for digital rights and campaign finance reform. He is best known for founding Creative Commons, a nonprofit that provides licenses to promote open access to creative works, empowering people to share and remix content legally. Lessig's career has focused on balancing intellectual property laws with the need for innovation in the digital age. His quote, *"Code is law,"* reflects his belief that the design of digital systems can shape freedom and behavior just as much as legislation.

Early Life: An Interest in Law and Public Policy

Born on June 3, 1961, in South Dakota, Lessig pursued a career in law and public policy, earning degrees from the University of Pennsylvania, Cambridge University, and Yale Law School. Early in his career, he clerked for Justice Antonin Scalia at the U.S. Supreme Court, gaining valuable insight into the judicial process. While Lessig initially focused on constitutional law, he later pivoted toward the intersection of law and technology.

Academic Success and Digital Activism

As a professor at institutions like Stanford and Harvard Law School, Lessig's work began to concentrate on how copyright laws were limiting creativity in the internet age. His groundbreaking book, "Free Culture" (2004), argued for reducing the restrictions on digital content to foster innovation and collaboration. In 2001, he co-founded Creative Commons, a revolutionary project that offered alternative copyright licenses to encourage the sharing of creative work.

Lessig is also known for his contributions to the concept of net neutrality and his advocacy against corporate influence in politics. His activism expanded into the political sphere with efforts to reform campaign finance laws through projects like Fix Congress First and the Mayday PAC.

Challenges and Campaign Finance Reform Advocacy

Lessig's fight against copyright monopolies and political corruption has faced significant challenges. Despite setbacks in his brief 2016 presidential campaign, his efforts continue to influence discussions on campaign finance reform and the dangers of corporate money in politics. His work remains influential in movements for transparency, open internet access, and fair elections.

Legacy: Advocating for Digital Freedom and Democracy

Through his academic work, activism, and public speaking, Lawrence Lessig has become a pioneer in the fight for a free and open internet. His contributions have shaped digital copyright policy, internet governance, and public discourse on campaign finance reform. Lessig's career exemplifies the importance of balancing innovation with legal frameworks, ensuring that democracy and creativity can thrive in a digital world.

Lessig's lifelong dedication to justice and freedom continues to inspire movements for open access, legal reform, and transparency, leaving a lasting legacy in both technology and public policy.

Leah Turner's Success Story: Elevating Conversations through Podcasting Strategy

"Podcasting is the modern-day campfire—around which we gather to tell our stories, share our experiences, and engage directly with our listeners, inviting them into the conversation." — LEAH TURNER, PODCAST STRATEGIST

Leah Turner is a podcast strategist and communications expert who has transformed the way individuals and organizations connect with audiences through the power of storytelling. Known for her philosophy that *"Podcasting is the modern-day campfire—around which we gather to tell our stories, share our experiences, and engage directly with our listeners, inviting them into the conversation,"* Turner emphasizes the role of authentic dialogue in building communities and fostering meaningful interactions.

Early Career: A Passion for Communication and Connection
Turner's career began with a background in communications and media, where she discovered the importance of storytelling as a tool to connect with audiences. With an innate understanding of content creation and audience engagement, she transitioned into the growing podcasting space, recognizing the platform's potential for intimate and direct communication.

Building a Podcasting Strategy Business
Turner founded her podcast strategy consulting business, working with brands, creators, and entrepreneurs to design podcasts that not only tell engaging stories but also align with business goals and audience needs. Her expertise lies in

helping clients craft authentic narratives, develop sustainable workflows, and leverage podcasting as a marketing tool to grow their influence.

Turner has worked on launching successful podcasts across industries, ensuring each show resonates with listeners through compelling content and consistent messaging. She focuses on creating conversational spaces where hosts can engage audiences as active participants rather than passive listeners.

Philosophy: Podcasting as Community-Building

Turner's approach to podcasting reflects her belief that podcasts are more than just content—they are spaces for dialogue and connection. She emphasizes that authentic conversations build trust and foster communities. Through strategic planning, Turner helps creators develop long-lasting relationships with listeners, transforming podcasts into valuable extensions of brands and businesses.

Legacy and Impact

Leah Turner's expertise in podcast strategy and storytelling has positioned her as a trusted leader in the industry. She continues to inspire podcasters to use their platforms intentionally, building communities around shared experiences and meaningful conversations. Turner's work serves as a blueprint for modern-day storytelling, demonstrating how strategic podcasting can elevate conversations and create lasting impact.

CHAPTER SIX

Crafting Stories That
Captivate Markets

In today's crowded business landscape, marketing messages are everywhere, making it increasingly difficult for companies to stand out. Storytelling offers a way to break through the noise and connect meaningfully with audiences. People respond to stories because they evoke emotion, build trust, and make brands relatable. This chapter explores the strategic use of storytelling in marketing and how it transforms products, services, and companies into experiences that customers want to engage with. Successful storytelling positions the audience as the hero of the narrative, with the brand acting as the guide that helps them overcome challenges and achieve their goals.

Some of the most powerful marketing campaigns weave compelling narratives about founders, customers, or the mission behind the brand. David Aaker, a branding expert, reminds us that "a strong brand story doesn't just tell what you do—it tells why it matters." Similarly, David Beebe, an expert in brand storytelling, advises that "brands need to stop interrupting what people are interested in and become what people are interested in." Storytelling is more than just sharing origin stories or testimonials—it can involve real-time interactions, social campaigns aligned with societal values, or playful narratives that capture attention in unexpected ways.

This chapter introduces key storytelling principles: authenticity, emotional resonance, relevance, and consistency. Elizabeth Gilbert, the acclaimed author of *Eat, Pray, Love*, emphasizes that storytelling must come from a place of truth, noting that "authenticity is what keeps people coming back." Stories need to align with your brand's mission and values, offering a genuine expression of what your business stands for. Emma Clarke, a voiceover artist known for her work on the London Underground, highlights the importance of understanding your audience's emotions, saying, "The most captivating stories are the ones that reflect the listener's journey." Stories that resonate emotionally create powerful connections, turning customers into loyal advocates.

Finding the right platform is essential for telling your story effectively. David Bowie, who revolutionized music and art through his storytelling personas, demonstrated how each medium requires a tailored approach. Whether through social media posts, video campaigns, podcasts, or email newsletters, every story should reflect your brand's identity and engage the audience. Diana Brooks, a creative consultant, adds, "Stories become meaningful when they fit the rhythm of the platform you're on." This chapter will help you identify which formats—Instagram visuals, blog posts, podcasts, or email campaigns—best suit your brand's message. The key is to ensure consistency across platforms while tailoring your storytelling style to the medium.

We will also explore how storytelling integrates into broader marketing strategies. Whether through branding campaigns or customer-centric content, stories allow companies to engage with authenticity and continuity. Joe Sugarcane, a digital marketer known for his work in viral campaigns, compares storytelling to "the spark that turns campaigns into movements." Meanwhile, Jane Friedman, an expert in publishing and digital storytelling, stresses that "great content is only effective if people can find it. SEO is the bridge between a good story and an audience." This chapter covers the technical side of storytelling, including how to ensure your narratives are discoverable through SEO and align seamlessly with your overall marketing goals.

At the heart of storytelling is the goal of building lasting relationships. David Aaker reminds us that "a great story builds loyalty by reflecting shared values and aspirations." Well-crafted stories not only capture attention but also enhance customer loyalty by reinforcing emotional connections. As Diana Brooks emphasizes, "A story without engagement is just noise—every story should invite interaction." Whether through comments, shares, or other forms of participation, storytelling fosters a sense of community that strengthens your brand.

By the end of this chapter, you will understand that storytelling is not just a creative pursuit—it's a strategic tool for cultivating loyalty and driving growth. Effective storytelling engages customers emotionally, turning them into advocates who amplify your message and deepen your brand's impact. With guidance from experts like David Beebe, Jane Friedman, and Elizabeth Gilbert, you will learn how to craft narratives that resonate and inspire action. Through storytelling, you transform your marketing from a series of disconnected messages into an ongoing conversation that builds community, trust, and long-term success.

═══════

David Aaker's Success Story: Pioneering the Art and Science of Branding

"Effective public relations doesn't just spread information—it seeds your brand's story in the public consciousness, growing an image that resonates and endures long after the initial buzz fades."
— DAVID AAKER, BRANDING EXPERT

David Aaker is a branding expert, author, and public relations strategist whose influential work has shaped how companies build and sustain brand identities. Known for his quote, *"Effective public relations doesn't just spread information—it seeds your brand's story in the public consciousness, growing an image that resonates and endures long after the initial buzz fades,"* Aaker emphasizes the importance of storytelling and brand consistency in building long-term recognition.

Early Career and Academic Foundations

Aaker began his career in academia, earning a Ph.D. from Stanford University and becoming a professor at the University of California, Berkeley's Haas School of Business. His early work focused on marketing and consumer behavior, leading him to explore the role of branding in business strategy. Over the years, Aaker developed some of the most influential frameworks in brand management, including the Aaker Brand Equity Model, which defines the value of a brand through awareness, loyalty, perceived quality, and brand associations.

Groundbreaking Thought Leadership in Branding

Through seminal books like "Building Strong Brands" and "Brand Leadership," Aaker provided companies with the tools to create strong brand identities that endure. His work introduced concepts such as brand equity and brand architecture, which have become essential components of modern marketing practices. Aaker argued that a brand is more than a name or logo—it is a set of perceptions and experiences that shape customer relationships.

His theories have helped companies worldwide understand how to leverage their brands for long-term success by aligning products, public relations strategies, and marketing initiatives under a cohesive brand story.

Public Relations Philosophy: Seeding Stories that Last

Aaker believes that effective public relations is about crafting narratives that embed a brand's identity within the public consciousness. His work highlights the importance of storytelling in shaping how brands are perceived and creating connections that extend beyond campaigns and buzz. Aaker emphasizes the need for consistency and authenticity in public messaging to ensure that a brand's story resonates and evolves meaningfully over time.

Legacy and Impact

Today, David Aaker is regarded as a pioneer in branding and marketing strategy, with his frameworks being taught in business schools and applied by global brands. His influence extends beyond marketing into corporate communication, public relations, and brand-building strategy, helping organizations craft identities that inspire trust and loyalty. Aaker's career exemplifies how strategic brand management can transform companies, creating icons that stand the test of time. His teachings continue to guide companies in building lasting narratives, shaping the future of brand-driven public relations and marketing.

David Bowie's Success Story: A Visionary Musician and Cultural Icon

"When dealing with copyright infringements, remember it's not just about defending your work; it's about upholding the respect for creativity itself." — DAVID BOWIE, MUSICIAN AND SONGWRITER

David Bowie was a musician, songwriter, and artist whose career spanned over five decades, marked by innovation, reinvention, and boundary-pushing creativity. Known for hits like *"Space Oddity," "Heroes,"* and *"Starman,"* Bowie became a cultural icon by embracing multiple artistic personas, such as Ziggy Stardust and The Thin White Duke. His work combined rock, glam, funk, electronic, and soul influences, often challenging societal norms and artistic conventions.

Early Life and Breakthrough Success

Bowie, born David Robert Jones in 1947 in London, developed an interest in music, art, and theater from a young age. In 1969, he gained widespread attention with his single "Space Oddity," which was released just days before the Apollo 11 moon landing. This early success set the stage for Bowie's unique career trajectory—one defined by continuous evolution and refusal to conform to industry expectations.

His breakthrough came with the creation of the Ziggy Stardust persona in 1972. The androgynous, otherworldly character became synonymous with Bowie's theatrical style and cemented his reputation as a musical pioneer, influencing generations of artists.

Musical Reinvention and Lasting Influence

Bowie's career was characterized by constant reinvention. From the soulful sound of Young Americans to the experimental Berlin Trilogy and the mainstream success of Let's Dance, Bowie embraced new genres and styles with every album. His ability to anticipate musical trends and reshape his identity ensured his relevance across decades.

Beyond his music, Bowie also pursued acting, starring in films such as The Man Who Fell to Earth and Labyrinth. His creative spirit extended into fashion, visual art, and cultural commentary, influencing not only music but also pop culture and identity politics.

Legacy and Intellectual Property Awareness

Bowie was also known for his savvy business acumen. In the 1990s, he pioneered the Bowie Bonds, a financial instrument that allowed him to leverage his music royalties—a groundbreaking move in music finance. Bowie's awareness of copyright and intellectual property informed his belief in the importance of protecting creative work. His quote, *"When dealing with copyright infringements, remember it's not just about defending your work; it's about upholding the respect for creativity itself,"* highlights his commitment to the integrity of artistic expression.

Final Chapter and Enduring Impact

Even in his final years, Bowie remained artistically active. His last album, Blackstar, was released just days before his death in 2016, a parting gift filled with introspection and innovation. His influence on music, fashion, art, and culture continues to resonate, as Bowie's work remains a testament to the power of reinvention, fearless creativity, and self-expression.

———————

Diana Brooks' Success Story: Orchestrating Success in Publishing

"Using a book aggregator is like hiring a symphony conductor for your publishing strategy; they harmonize your book's presence across multiple platforms, ensuring it reaches every corner of the audience without missing a beat." — DIANA BROOKS, PUBLISHING CONSULTANT

Diana Brooks is a publishing consultant and expert in book distribution strategy, known for helping authors and publishers optimize their reach across multiple platforms. Her philosophy, *"Using a book aggregator is like hiring a symphony conductor for your publishing strategy; they harmonize your book's presence across multiple platforms, ensuring it reaches every corner of the audience without missing a beat,"* reflects her focus on strategic coordination and distribution excellence.

Early Career: A Passion for Publishing

Brooks began her career in editorial roles with traditional publishers, gaining hands-on experience in manuscript development and market analysis. This foundation gave her a keen understanding of the challenges authors face—not only in writing great books but also in getting them into the hands of readers.

As digital publishing platforms emerged, Brooks identified an opportunity to bridge the gap between content creation and distribution. She recognized the power of book aggregators, which allow authors to publish across multiple digital platforms efficiently. Her expertise in distribution management and metadata optimization soon made her a sought-after consultant in the industry.

Building a Consultancy: Guiding Authors to Success

With years of experience under her belt, Brooks launched her own publishing consultancy, helping authors and independent publishers navigate the complexities of the digital landscape. She focuses on aggregator platforms that distribute books to retailers such as Amazon, Apple Books, and Kobo, ensuring that authors can maximize their visibility and sales potential.

Brooks provides tailored strategies for self-published authors, guiding them through ISBN management, pricing models, and market positioning. She also emphasizes the importance of metadata alignment, ensuring that each book is searchable and optimized for various platforms.

A Thought Leader in Modern Publishing

As a thought leader, Brooks emphasizes that distribution is as important as content in a competitive publishing environment. Her consulting work helps authors streamline workflows, focusing not only on where books are published but how they are marketed and discovered. She believes in harmonizing creativity with strategy, ensuring that every book launch is coordinated across channels for maximum impact.

Legacy: Empowering Authors and Publishers

Diana Brooks continues to inspire authors to take control of their publishing journeys through education, consulting, and practical strategies. Her work empowers clients to leverage technology and distribution tools, transforming great books into global successes. By bridging creativity with logistical expertise, Brooks ensures that her clients not only publish but thrive in today's dynamic publishing landscape.

Elizabeth Gilbert's Success Story: From Struggling Writer to Literary Icon

"Book clubs are not just about sharing books; they're about sharing stories and experiences that turn individual readers into a powerful collective of advocates." — ELIZABETH GILBERT, ACCLAIMED AUTHOR

Elizabeth Gilbert is a renowned author and speaker, best known for her memoir "Eat, Pray, Love," which became a global bestseller and cultural phenomenon. Her journey to success reflects persistence, creativity, and deep introspection. Before her breakthrough, Gilbert worked as a journalist and short story writer, with early struggles shaping her unique voice and literary style.

Early Career and Breakthrough

Born in 1969 in Connecticut, Gilbert attended New York University before embarking on a career as a writer. She gained recognition for her journalistic work, with pieces published in GQ and The New York Times Magazine. Gilbert's early career included the release of her short story collection, "Pilgrims," which was well-received but didn't achieve mainstream success.

Her breakthrough came in 2006 with the release of "Eat, Pray, Love," a memoir about personal rediscovery and travel following a difficult divorce. The book struck a chord with readers, spending over 200 weeks on The New York Times bestseller list and becoming a hit film starring Julia Roberts. Gilbert's ability to weave personal stories into universal themes captivated a global audience, making her an influential voice in literature and self-reflection.

Philosophy: Sharing Stories and Experiences

Gilbert's quote, *"Book clubs are not just about sharing books; they're about sharing stories and experiences that turn individual readers into a powerful collective of advocates,"* reflects her deep understanding of the transformative power of stories. She believes that books are not merely solitary experiences but vehicles for connection and community.

Through her novels, essays, and memoirs, Gilbert explores themes of self-discovery, creativity, and personal growth. In her book "Big Magic: Creative Living Beyond Fear," she encourages readers to embrace curiosity and fearlessness in creative endeavors. Her writing offers insight into overcoming doubt, embracing imperfection, and finding meaning through creative expression.

Impact and Legacy

Today, Elizabeth Gilbert remains a beloved author and speaker, influencing readers with her engaging storytelling and candid reflections on life's challenges. Beyond her memoirs, she has written works of fiction, essays, and self-help, continually evolving as both an author and thought leader. Her ability to inspire individuals to embrace their journeys, find beauty in struggles, and connect through shared stories ensures that her work continues to resonate with book clubs and readers worldwide.

Gilbert's legacy demonstrates the power of authenticity and vulnerability in storytelling, offering readers a sense of hope, empowerment, and community.

―――――――

Emma Clarke's Success Story: Crafting Stories through the Magic of Voice

"Audiobooks aren't just about reading aloud; they're an invitation to experience stories through the intimate magic of voice, turning listeners into vivid participants in the narrative journey." — EMMA CLARKE, AUDIOBOOK PRODUCER

Emma Clarke is a renowned audiobook producer and voice artist, celebrated for her ability to transform written stories into immersive audio experiences. Her philosophy, *"Audiobooks aren't just about reading aloud; they're an invitation to experience stories through the intimate magic of voice, turning listeners into vivid participants in the narrative journey,"* reflects her deep understanding of how voice brings stories to life.

Early Career: Finding a Voice in Audio Production
Clarke's journey began with a background in radio broadcasting and voiceover work, where she discovered the impact of voice in storytelling. Her work in radio cultivated her skills in vocal nuance and timing, which would later play a crucial role in her transition to audiobook production. Clarke developed a passion for creating audio content that goes beyond simple narration, focusing on the emotional depth and subtleties that a good performance can convey.

Building a Career in Audiobook Production
With the rise of digital platforms, Clarke shifted her focus to audiobook production, helping authors and publishers translate their works into audio formats. Her ability to guide voice talent and direct immersive audio experiences quickly made her a sought-after producer. Clarke's projects span genres, from fiction to nonfiction, ensuring that every audiobook resonates with listeners on a personal and emotional level.

Clarke emphasizes the importance of casting the right narrator and balancing sound design with the narrative's tone, making each production a unique auditory experience. She also works closely with authors and publishers, ensuring that the essence of the story is faithfully conveyed through voice.

Philosophy: Voice as a Narrative Tool

For Clarke, audiobooks represent more than just an alternative to reading—they provide an intimate way to experience stories. She sees each listener as a participant in the storytelling process, transported by the emotions, pacing, and delivery of the narrator. Her approach emphasizes precision in voice work and emotional resonance, ensuring that listeners are fully immersed in the narrative journey.

Legacy and Impact

Emma Clarke's work has contributed to the growing popularity of audiobooks, especially in the era of streaming services and digital libraries. Her focus on quality production and meaningful engagement has helped raise the standards for audiobook experiences, earning her acclaim in the publishing industry. Clarke's legacy reflects a commitment to crafting stories with voice, demonstrating how sound can enrich the reading experience and invite listeners into new worlds.

Joe Sugarman's Success Story: The Copywriting Legend Who Transformed Advertising

"A great pitch isn't just about presenting ideas; it's about making your audience feel they can't afford to miss out." — JOE SUGARMAN, ADVERTISING EXPERT

Joe Sugarman was a trailblazing entrepreneur, copywriter, and marketing genius, known for revolutionizing direct response advertising. His innovative, customer-focused approach to sales copy and advertising techniques not only built his own companies but also influenced generations of marketers. Sugarman's journey from selling gadgets through mail-order catalogs to becoming a legend in the world of copywriting is a story of vision, creativity, and resilience.

Early Life and Military Beginnings

Joe Sugarman was born in Chicago, Illinois, in 1938. He grew up in a working-class family, which fostered his strong work ethic and entrepreneurial spirit. After high school, Sugarman attended the University of Miami, but his education was interrupted by military service. He served as an Air Force electronics officer during the Vietnam War, which gave him exposure to cutting-edge technology.

Upon returning home, Sugarman found himself drawn to the world of business. However, it wasn't an easy start—he struggled to find his footing and had a few false starts with small business ventures.

The Birth of JS&A: A Mail-Order Catalog Empire

Sugarman's entrepreneurial breakthrough came when he launched JS&A Group in 1969, a mail-order business selling high-tech gadgets and electronics through catalogs and print ads. The company became known for selling products like pocket calculators, cordless phones, and digital watches—technologies that were cutting-edge at the time. However, it wasn't just the products that made JS&A a success—it was Sugarman's revolutionary approach to marketing.

Sugarman began experimenting with long-form print ads, packed with engaging storytelling, humor, and insights. His ads were personal and conversational, standing out from the dry, transactional ads of the era. He believed in educating the customer and building trust through authentic storytelling—an approach that made his products feel irresistible to readers.

The BluBlocker Sunglasses Phenomenon

One of Sugarman's most famous successes was BluBlocker Sunglasses. While on vacation, he tested a pair of sunglasses that filtered out blue light, providing crystal-clear vision. Recognizing the product's potential, Sugarman used his copywriting magic to turn BluBlockers into a global sensation.

His long-form TV ads and infomercials for BluBlockers were just as engaging as his print ads. Sugarman's storytelling and personable delivery connected with audiences, making the sunglasses not just a product, but a lifestyle. BluBlockers went on to sell millions of units and remain a recognizable brand to this day.

The Copywriting Secrets That Made Sugarman a Legend

Sugarman's philosophy on copywriting was groundbreaking. He believed that a good piece of copy should create a "slippery slope"—a sense of flow that carries the reader from the headline to the very last sentence without interruption. He taught that engagement, trust, and emotional resonance were far more important than hard-sell tactics.

Sugarman shared his secrets in "The Adweek Copywriting Handbook," a book that has become a bible for marketers and copywriters worldwide. In the book, Sugarman outlined practical strategies, including:

1. The power of curiosity in headlines.

2. Building trust through storytelling.

3. Creating irresistible offers.

4. Anticipating and addressing customer objections within the copy.

His insights revolutionized how direct-response ads were written, inspiring an entire generation of copywriters to focus on empathy, storytelling, and engagement.

Adapting to Changing Times

While JS&A Group thrived for years, the company eventually faced challenges as new technologies emerged and consumer habits shifted. Sugarman's ability to pivot and adapt kept him relevant even in an evolving marketplace. He ventured into infomercials, where his BluBlocker campaigns became iconic, and embraced new forms of media marketing, always staying ahead of the curve.

Sugarman's ability to combine timeless principles of copywriting with evolving media platforms became the hallmark of his career. He understood that human nature—the emotions, motivations, and desires that drive purchases—remained constant, even as technologies changed.

Legacy: Teaching the Next Generation of Marketers

As he transitioned out of day-to-day business operations, Sugarman dedicated himself to teaching and mentoring. He became a sought-after speaker at marketing events, sharing his insights and inspiring entrepreneurs and marketers around the world. His books, workshops, and courses have influenced some of the biggest names in modern marketing.

Sugarman believed in giving back, helping others achieve success by sharing everything he had learned. His teaching style—informal, insightful, and entertaining—made complex marketing concepts easy to understand. He was known for his generosity with advice, often reminding students that success in marketing comes from building trust and relationships.

Lessons from Joe Sugarman's Success

Sugarman's career offers a number of powerful lessons for aspiring entrepreneurs and marketers:

- **Educate, don't just sell.** Customers are more likely to buy when they feel informed and empowered.

- **Storytelling builds trust.** People are more likely to engage with a product if they connect emotionally to the story behind it.

- **Curiosity drives action.** A great headline grabs attention by sparking curiosity, pulling the reader into the ad.

- **Adapt to changing times.** Staying relevant requires embracing new technologies and evolving strategies without losing sight of fundamental principles.

Conclusion: A Legacy of Innovation and Trust

Joe Sugarman's journey from an Air Force officer to a marketing legend is a testament to the power of creativity, persistence, and empathy. His ability to blend storytelling with sales strategies not only built a successful business but also transformed the world of advertising.

Sugarman's legacy lives on through the countless entrepreneurs, marketers, and copywriters who have applied his principles to grow their own businesses. His story serves as a reminder that success isn't just about making sales—it's about building relationships, creating value, and sharing stories that resonate with people.

With his innovative mindset and unwavering commitment to authentic communication, Joe Sugarman left an indelible mark on the marketing world—

proving that the right words, delivered with the right intent, can change everything.

Jane Friedman's Success Story: A Leader in Publishing and Author Empowerment

"Our author website is your greatest marketing tool. Treat it like a garden; tend it carefully, make it beautiful and functional, and people will want to return again and again." — JANE FRIEDMAN, PUBLISHING EXPERT AND AUTHOR

Jane Friedman is a publishing expert, author, and educator known for helping writers navigate the evolving world of traditional and self-publishing. Her quote, *"Your author website is your greatest marketing tool. Treat it like a garden; tend it carefully, make it beautiful and functional, and people will want to return again and again,"* reflects her philosophy on the importance of digital presence and author branding.

Early Career: A Foundation in Publishing

Friedman's career began with leadership roles in traditional publishing, including her work as the Publisher and Editorial Director at Writer's Digest. During her tenure, she gained invaluable experience in writing, editing, and industry trends, building a deep understanding of the challenges authors face.

As digital platforms started reshaping the publishing landscape, Friedman recognized the opportunity for authors to take control of their careers by leveraging online tools and platforms. This realization prompted her to transition into teaching and consulting, where she began focusing on author education, marketing, and platform building.

Building a Career in Author Education and Consulting

Friedman established herself as a leading voice in the publishing world through her courses, consulting, and public speaking engagements. Her website, JaneFriedman.com, became a hub for practical advice, offering guidance on query letters, book marketing, publishing strategies, and digital tools. She emphasizes long-term, sustainable career planning, helping authors navigate both traditional and self-publishing pathways.

In addition to consulting, Friedman authored several books, including "The Business of Being a Writer," which is widely regarded as an essential resource for understanding the economics of publishing. Her ability to demystify the business side of writing makes her a trusted mentor to aspiring and established authors alike.

Philosophy: Empowering Authors through Knowledge

Friedman believes in the importance of building a personal brand and maintaining an engaging online presence, with the author website serving as the foundation. Her philosophy encourages writers to invest in their platforms, treating them as spaces where readers feel welcomed and engaged. This approach aligns with her broader vision of empowering authors to take control of their marketing and career trajectories.

Legacy and Influence

Jane Friedman has become a go-to resource for authors, publishers, and industry professionals seeking practical, actionable advice. Her work bridges the gap between traditional publishing expertise and digital innovation, making her an influential figure in author education and publishing consulting. Her impact can be seen in the countless authors she has mentored, empowering them to succeed in a changing publishing landscape through knowledge, strategy, and creativity.

David Beebe's Success Story: A Pioneer in Content Marketing and Branded Entertainment

"Conquering the world of online magazines and e-zines isn't just about making noise; it's about making a mark—creating content that resonates deeply and persists long after the browser window closes." — DAVID BEEBE, CONTENT MARKETING EXECUTIVE

David Beebe is a content marketing executive, producer, and digital strategist whose career has transformed the way brands create and distribute content.

Known for his quote, *"Conquering the world of online magazines and e-zines isn't just about making noise; it's about making a mark—creating content that resonates deeply and persists long after the browser window closes,"* Beebe emphasizes the importance of storytelling that leaves a lasting impact. His journey from television production to becoming a leader in content marketing reflects his ability to merge creativity and commerce, redefining how companies connect with audiences.

Early Life and Beginnings in Television Production
Beebe's career began in the world of television and entertainment, where he developed a passion for narrative storytelling. Working with networks like ABC and Showtime, Beebe honed his ability to create content that engages emotionally with viewers. His work in television introduced him to the art of crafting stories that capture attention and build connections, skills he would later apply to branded entertainment.

This early experience taught Beebe that content must be meaningful to last, a philosophy that would guide him as he transitioned into digital content and marketing strategy.

Pioneering Branded Entertainment at Marriott
Beebe's most notable role came when he joined Marriott International, where he launched and led the Marriott Content Studio. At Marriott, Beebe was at the forefront of branded entertainment, producing travel-focused web series, short films, and documentaries that didn't just promote the brand but told engaging, human stories. This innovative approach blurred the line between entertainment and advertising, offering consumers content they wanted to watch rather than ads they tried to avoid.

His campaigns, such as Two Bellmen and The Navigator Live, became industry benchmarks, illustrating how storytelling could drive brand loyalty and engagement. Beebe's work at Marriott proved that creating entertaining content aligned with a brand's identity could generate both emotional connection and business value.

Expanding Influence in Content Strategy

Following his success at Marriott, Beebe expanded his influence as a consultant, speaker, and thought leader in content marketing. He began working with companies and brands across industries, teaching them how to leverage storytelling as a key component of their digital strategy. His expertise spans not only video production and branded content but also the role of e-zines and online magazines in building sustainable brand identities.

Beebe's work focuses on the idea that content must inform, inspire, and endure. He advocates for creating digital experiences that resonate with audiences long after their initial interaction, believing that consistent, meaningful storytelling is the key to lasting engagement.

Philosophy: Building Stories that Last Beyond the Buzz

Beebe's approach to content creation is deeply rooted in authenticity and emotional resonance. His quote about e-zines and online content reflects his understanding that temporary trends fade, but stories that connect on a human level create loyal brand advocates. Beebe encourages brands to treat their digital presence as more than just noise-making channels—they must seed narratives into the public consciousness that inspire action and foster relationships.

Legacy and Continued Impact

Today, David Beebe remains a leading voice in content marketing, continuing to educate brands, marketers, and entrepreneurs on the importance of strategic storytelling. Through his consulting work, public speaking, and content production, he helps organizations harness the power of narrative to achieve both business goals and emotional impact.

His ability to merge art with commerce, whether through online magazines, branded films, or podcasts, has changed how companies think about content. Beebe's legacy in branded entertainment and digital storytelling continues to shape the future of content marketing, proving that the right story, told in the right way, can make an enduring impact.

───────

CHAPTER SEVEN

Expanding Reach with Digital Communities

In the digital age, building an online audience is both an art and a science. Successful businesses thrive by engaging with the right people in the right places, transforming casual visitors into loyal supporters. Creating a thriving community is not just about increasing numbers—it's about fostering meaningful relationships with individuals who believe in your brand, interact with your content, and become powerful advocates. This chapter explores how to strategically cultivate and grow your online audience using content, social media, and digital marketing tools.

Alvin Adams, known for his diplomatic skills, said, "Building relationships is about making connections that transcend transactions." In the same way, building a digital community requires creating an environment where every interaction adds value and every member feels they belong. Whether you start with a blog, social media presence, or website, the goal is to build meaningful connections that go beyond mere marketing. Joe Chernov, a content marketing expert, advises, "The best content doesn't just speak for a brand—it speaks with the audience."

Understanding where your ideal audience gathers and what they care about is critical to building an engaged community. Mia Caldwell, an expert in engagement strategies, emphasizes, "Content is only part of the equation—real engagement happens through authentic interaction." It's not enough to create compelling content; fostering conversation and responding to comments consistently is just as important. Platforms like LinkedIn, which Rebecca Grant calls "a global marketplace of thought leadership," offer valuable opportunities for building connections and establishing authority. Similarly, Leslie Turner advises that, "Social media success lies not in broadcasting messages but in creating moments that compel people to engage."

Consistency is a key component in building a strong online following. Jenna Atkinson, a personal branding coach, notes that "Consistency builds credibility, and credibility builds trust." This chapter explores how maintaining a consistent voice and presence across platforms helps your audience stay connected with your brand. From blog posts to Instagram stories, every piece of content contributes to building a relationship that lasts. Elizabeth Grant, an expert in digital storytelling, adds, "Your content should not only reflect your values but also align with what your audience cares about."

Beyond creating content, technical strategies like SEO play a crucial role in audience growth. Rob Kalin, co-founder of Etsy, reminds us that "Great content only matters if people can find it." Optimizing your blog posts, social media updates, and website ensures that your message reaches the right people. Rebecca Grant emphasizes that SEO is about more than search rankings—it's about connecting with people who are looking for exactly what you offer.

Flexibility is also essential when building a digital audience. Leslie Turner notes that, "The digital landscape evolves quickly, and brands must evolve with it." This chapter discusses how to adjust your strategies based on analytics and audience feedback. Whether you're experimenting with Pinterest's visual storytelling or building relationships through podcasts, adaptability is key to long-term growth. Elizabeth Grant highlights the power of visual platforms: "Images tell stories that words can't, drawing your audience deeper into your brand's narrative."

Building an audience is not just about numbers; it's about creating meaningful connections. Alvin Adams said, "A network is not just a list of names; it's a web of potential relationships waiting to be activated." Whether through newsletters, social media, or blogs, your goal should be to foster interactions that build trust and loyalty. Mia Caldwell adds, "Podcasting is like sitting down for coffee with your audience—one conversation at a time."

This chapter offers strategies for building and nurturing an online audience that goes beyond surface-level engagement. With insights from Joe Chernov, Jenna Atkinson, and Mia Caldwell, you'll learn how to align your messaging, engage authentically, and remain consistent in your digital efforts. By building a strong, connected community around your brand, you'll not only attract loyal customers but also inspire them to share your message, helping your business grow and thrive in the long run. Through meaningful storytelling and authentic engagement, you'll turn followers into advocates and create a digital community that fuels sustainable success.

Alvin Adams's Success Story: Forging the path for American Express and Modern Logistics

"Public relations are a key component of any operation in this day of instant communications and rightly inquisitive citizens." — ALVIN ADAMS, FOUNDER OF THE AMERICAN EXPRESS COMPANY

Alvin Adams was a visionary entrepreneur who helped shape the American logistics industry in the 19th century through his company, Adams and Company, a forerunner to American Express. His pioneering work in express delivery laid the foundation for secure, reliable shipping networks and inspired future giants in financial services and transportation. Adams's success demonstrates the power of resilience, customer service, and operational efficiency in building lasting enterprises during a time of economic expansion and technological change.

Early Life: Finding Opportunity in Chaos

Born in Andover, Vermont, in 1804, Alvin Adams experienced early business failure during the Panic of 1837, a devastating financial crisis that affected merchants nationwide. When his produce business collapsed, Adams saw an opportunity in a growing but underdeveloped sector: express shipping. At that time, the U.S. postal system was slow, unreliable, and ill-equipped to handle urgent deliveries of money, goods, and documents. Adams recognized the potential for private express services to bridge this gap.

The Founding of Adams and Company

In 1840, Adams launched his express delivery service between Boston and New York, using a small network of stagecoaches and railways to transport valuable items, packages, and banknotes. His business was built on the principle of speed, reliability, and customer trust, with an emphasis on delivering secure financial documents and goods for merchants and banks. The company quickly expanded, adding routes to Philadelphia, Baltimore, and Washington, D.C., and became essential to American commerce during this period of urbanization and economic growth.

Adams and Company thrived by partnering with financial institutions and other businesses, ensuring timely and secure delivery services. These partnerships allowed Adams to build trust and expand his operations across the Northeast, gaining a reputation as a reliable alternative to government mail services.

Expanding the Express Industry

As Adams and Company grew, Alvin Adams and his competitors transformed express shipping from a niche service to a vital part of the American economy. His efforts contributed to the standardization of parcel delivery, including establishing a uniform pricing model that would later inspire postal reforms. Adams was instrumental in creating a delivery system that was accessible and affordable, offering businesses and individuals a more efficient way to transport goods and documents.

The Rise of American Express

While Adams was building his express empire, other leaders in the field—including Henry Wells and William G. Fargo—were also expanding their services. In 1850, Adams's competitors merged their operations to form the

American Express Company, consolidating express routes across the northeastern United States. Although Adams and Company did not join the merger, Alvin Adams's influence on the express industry profoundly shaped how companies like American Express and Wells Fargo operated, particularly in their emphasis on trust, security, and customer service.

American Express quickly became known for its ability to transport high-value items safely and reliably, reflecting the standards that Adams had set. His pioneering business model laid the groundwork for the expansion of American Express into financial services in later years.

Legacy: A Lasting Impact on Logistics and Finance

Even though Alvin Adams's company did not merge into American Express, his role in modernizing express shipping remains significant. Adams Express, the successor to his original company, continued to operate as a key player in logistics well into the 20th century. Meanwhile, American Express evolved from a regional express service into a global financial institution, applying the principles Adams had pioneered: trust, efficiency, and customer-first service.

Adams's work also set the standard for public relations and customer interaction within logistics. His philosophy emphasized the importance of clear communication with clients and maintaining public trust—a principle embodied in his belief that express services were essential to the smooth functioning of the economy. His foresight helped transform express delivery from a localized industry into a nationwide enterprise, creating the conditions for technological advancements and global financial networks.

Conclusion: Alvin Adams's Enduring Legacy

Alvin Adams's story is one of perseverance, innovation, and strategic foresight. From the collapse of his produce business to the founding of Adams and Company, Adams's ability to adapt and seize opportunities during times of uncertainty allowed him to redefine express services in the United States. His influence can still be felt today, as his business practices shaped the development of modern financial logistics.

Though not directly involved in the founding of American Express, Adams's innovations and business principles were crucial in inspiring the growth of express delivery companies that ultimately transformed into some of the world's largest financial institutions. His life exemplifies how visionary thinking and a commitment to reliability can lay the foundation for long-term success and industry-wide change.

Joe Chernov's Success Story: A Trailblazer in Marketing and Content Strategy

"Good marketing makes the company look smart. Great marketing makes the customer feel smart." — JOE CHERNOV, MARKETING EXECUTIVE AND THOUGHT LEADER

Joe Chernov is a marketing executive, speaker, and thought leader known for his innovative approach to content marketing and brand storytelling. With the philosophy, *"Good marketing makes the company look smart. Great marketing makes the customer feel smart,"* Chernov has championed customer-focused marketing strategies throughout his career, helping organizations engage their audiences in meaningful ways. His work has been instrumental in shaping modern content marketing, establishing him as one of the leading voices in the industry.

Early Career: Building a Foundation in Marketing

Chernov's career began in public relations and corporate communications, where he developed skills in strategic messaging, media relations, and brand management. Early in his career, he recognized the shift towards customer-centric marketing, where businesses needed to offer valuable content rather than simply broadcasting promotional messages. His experiences laid the groundwork for his focus on building content strategies that empower customers while achieving business objectives.

Chernov's breakthrough came when he embraced content marketing as a core business function—a relatively new concept at the time. His ability to combine storytelling with data-driven insights enabled him to create engaging campaigns that resonated with customers while delivering tangible results for companies.

Making His Mark: HubSpot and Eloqua

Chernov made significant contributions as a marketing leader at Eloqua, a pioneer in marketing automation software. While at Eloqua, he built one of the most recognized content marketing programs in the B2B space, setting a standard for how SaaS companies can use content to drive engagement and educate customers. Under Chernov's leadership, the company became a thought leader in marketing automation, and his efforts played a critical role in Eloqua's successful IPO and acquisition by Oracle.

Following his success at Eloqua, Chernov took on leadership roles at HubSpot, another content marketing powerhouse. At HubSpot, he helped refine the company's inbound marketing strategy, leveraging blogs, e-books, whitepapers, and webinars to attract and engage customers. HubSpot's content-driven approach became a model for other companies, and Chernov's work there solidified his reputation as a content marketing pioneer.

Philosophy: Customer-Centered Marketing

Chernov's quote—*"Good marketing makes the company look smart. Great marketing makes the customer feel smart"*—encapsulates his belief in empowering customers through marketing. He advocates for creating content that adds value to the audience, helping them solve problems, learn new skills, or make informed decisions. For Chernov, the key to effective marketing lies in earning trust and building relationships through content that resonates with customers on a personal level.

Impact and Legacy: A Leader in Modern Marketing

Chernov's influence extends beyond the companies he has worked for. He is a sought-after speaker and advisor, frequently sharing insights on content marketing, brand storytelling, and customer engagement at industry conferences. His thought leadership has shaped how businesses approach content marketing strategies, helping companies understand that success comes from putting the customer first.

Today, Joe Chernov continues to inspire marketing professionals and executives, encouraging them to adopt customer-centric mindsets and invest in meaningful content. His career is a testament to the power of strategic content marketing, showing how engaging storytelling and practical insights can create lasting relationships between brands and customers.

Jenna Atkinson's Success Story: Empowering Growth through Marketing Strategy

"In marketing, a picture isn't just worth a thousand words; it's worth a thousand clicks, a thousand shares, and potentially a thousand sales."

— JENNA ATKINSON, MARKETING STRATEGIST

Jenna Atkinson is a marketing strategist, entrepreneur, and motivational speaker, known for her ability to transform brands and individuals through strategic marketing, business development, and personal growth programs. Her quote, *"In marketing, a picture isn't just worth a thousand words; it's worth a thousand clicks, a thousand shares, and potentially a thousand sales,"* embodies her belief in the power of visual storytelling and engagement-driven marketing strategies. Atkinson's work is dedicated to helping professionals build meaningful connections and sustainable business success through smart marketing initiatives.

Early Life and Professional Growth

Atkinson's career began with a passion for communications and leadership development. After studying business and marketing, she quickly recognized the potential of digital marketing platforms and social media tools in building personal brands and helping businesses scale. Early in her career, she worked with entrepreneurs and small businesses, identifying the challenges they faced in establishing their presence in competitive markets. These experiences helped her develop a customer-focused marketing approach that emphasized visual engagement and long-term brand loyalty.

Atkinson's background in coaching and leadership gave her a unique perspective on personal development, influencing her marketing philosophy. She believes in holistic strategies—where business goals align with individual purpose and passion—making her work particularly resonant with professionals seeking to grow their influence and impact in the marketplace.

Building The P5 Project: Empowering Women for Success

In pursuit of her mission to create lasting impact, Atkinson founded The P5 Project, a platform focused on helping women increase their income, impact, and influence. The project's name reflects the five core areas of professional growth that Atkinson emphasizes: purpose, passion, persistence, profitability, and power. Through this initiative, she provides workshops, coaching, and networking opportunities aimed at equipping women with the tools to excel in leadership roles and build thriving businesses.

Her expertise lies not just in marketing techniques but in understanding how personal branding can open doors for professional success. Atkinson's programs guide participants in leveraging social media and content marketing tools, turning every visual or post into an opportunity for meaningful engagement and business growth.

Podcasting and Thought Leadership: The Growth Bomb Podcast

Atkinson also hosts The Growth Bomb Podcast, a platform where she shares insights on entrepreneurship, personal development, and business growth. In each episode, Atkinson interviews successful entrepreneurs and thought leaders, distilling actionable advice on how to build momentum and achieve breakthroughs in business. The podcast reflects her belief that learning from others' journeys is essential for personal and professional development, inspiring listeners to take action and seize opportunities.

Atkinson's work as a podcast host has earned her a reputation as a thought leader in marketing and business development, helping individuals and businesses unlock their potential through intentional strategies.

Marketing Philosophy: Turning Stories into Sales

Jenna Atkinson's marketing philosophy revolves around customer engagement through storytelling and visual content. For her, marketing is not just about promoting products—it's about creating connections that inspire trust and loyalty. She encourages businesses to integrate visual storytelling into their strategies, ensuring that each piece of content has the potential to engage audiences and generate measurable results.

Her quote, *"A picture isn't just worth a thousand words; it's worth a thousand clicks, a thousand shares, and potentially a thousand sales,"* encapsulates her belief in the power of imagery and thoughtful messaging in driving business success. Whether it's a social media post or a campaign launch, Atkinson emphasizes that every touchpoint must resonate with audiences and inspire action.

Impact and Legacy: Recognitions and Influence

Atkinson's work has earned her several accolades, including being named one of the 40 Under 40 and nominated for the Athena Young Professional Award. These recognitions reflect her commitment to leadership, mentorship, and community building, particularly in helping women and entrepreneurs achieve financial and personal success.

Her efforts go beyond business growth; Atkinson is passionate about empowering individuals to align their personal values with professional goals. She inspires her clients and audiences to think beyond profits and focus on building sustainable legacies that reflect their purpose and passions.

Conclusion: A Legacy of Empowerment and Engagement

Jenna Atkinson's journey from business strategist to influential thought leader demonstrates how marketing, when done right, can be a force for empowerment and transformation. Through The P5 Project, her podcast, and her marketing consultancy, she continues to inspire individuals and organizations to unlock their potential through smart strategies and authentic storytelling. Her focus on visual engagement, customer-centric marketing, and personal development has made her a respected figure in the world of business growth and leadership.

Atkinson's work reflects her belief that marketing is about more than just making noise—it's about creating connections that inspire action, foster relationships, and build lasting success.

———————

Mia Caldwell's Bringing Stories to Life through Animation

"Animation isn't just for cartoons. It's the magic that turns static images into stories that move both literally and figuratively, capturing the heart of the viewer and refusing to let go." — MIA CALDWELL, DIGITAL MEDIA EXPERT

Mia Caldwell is a digital media expert and animation specialist whose work transforms static visuals into dynamic storytelling experiences. Known for her quote, *"Animation isn't just for cartoons. It's the magic that turns static images into stories that move both literally and figuratively, capturing the heart of the viewer and refusing to let go,"* Caldwell emphasizes the emotional power of movement in digital storytelling.

Early Career: From Design to Digital Media
Caldwell's career began with a passion for visual design and media arts, where she experimented with combining graphic elements and animation. As the demand for interactive and digital content grew, Caldwell recognized animation's potential to engage audiences in new ways. She shifted her focus from static graphic design to motion graphics and animation, mastering tools like Adobe After Effects, Blender, and Maya to bring her creative visions to life.

Her early work involved collaborations with small studios and digital agencies, producing animated content for advertising campaigns and educational platforms. These projects showcased Caldwell's ability to blend storytelling with technical precision, making even complex narratives engaging and accessible.

Building a Career in Animation and Digital Storytelling
As Caldwell's expertise grew, she took on leadership roles in digital media production, guiding teams through full-scale animation projects. She worked with media companies and content creators to develop animated features, explainer videos, and interactive content for websites and mobile platforms. Her versatility allowed her to transition smoothly between 2D and 3D animation, giving her the creative freedom to meet the needs of various industries.

Caldwell's deep understanding of audience engagement led her to explore interactive media, combining animation with user experiences (UX) and augmented reality (AR) to create immersive content. Her projects reflected her philosophy that animation isn't limited to entertainment—it's a tool that can convey emotions, ideas, and messages across any medium.

Philosophy: Animation as an Emotional Connector

Mia Caldwell's approach to animation reflects her belief that motion has the power to connect emotionally with viewers. For Caldwell, animation is not just about technical skills—it's about crafting stories that resonate and stay with the audience. Her projects emphasize visual storytelling, where each frame contributes to the emotional impact of the narrative.

She has often said that successful animation is about movement that makes meaning, whether it's a character's subtle expression or a symbolic transition between scenes. Caldwell teaches that every animated element should serve the story, making the viewer feel connected and engaged with the content on a deeper level.

Impact and Legacy: Empowering the Next Generation of Animators

Mia Caldwell's influence extends beyond her personal projects. She actively mentors young animators and digital artists, helping them harness the power of animation to tell compelling stories. Through workshops and online courses, Caldwell shares her insights into digital media production, animation workflows, and storytelling techniques, inspiring the next generation of creatives to push the boundaries of visual storytelling.

Her work has been featured in commercials, online courses, web series, and mobile apps, demonstrating the versatility of animation in marketing, education, and entertainment. Caldwell's passion for animation has made her a thought leader in the digital media space, where her insights continue to shape how brands and creators communicate with audiences.

Conclusion: Shaping the Future of Digital Media

Mia Caldwell's journey from visual design to digital animation exemplifies the power of creativity, passion, and storytelling. Through her work, she demonstrates that animation is more than just moving images—it's a way to capture hearts, convey ideas, and inspire action. Her career has been defined by a commitment to innovation and emotional engagement, proving that animation can thrive in marketing, education, and immersive experiences alike.

Caldwell's legacy lies in her ability to teach and inspire. Whether working with brands or mentoring new artists, she continues to push the boundaries of what animation can achieve, ensuring that her work and influence remain impactful in the evolving world of digital media.

Rebecca Grant's Success Story: Turning Bookstores into Story Stages

"Partnering with booksellers isn't just about getting your book on the shelf—it's about turning each bookstore into a stage where your story can truly shine and captivate the audience." — REBECCA GRANT, AUTHOR AND MARKETING EXPERT

Rebecca Grant is a marketing expert and author, known for her innovative approach to book marketing and author-brand partnerships. Her quote, *"Partnering with booksellers isn't just about getting your book on the shelf—it's about turning each bookstore into a stage where your story can truly shine and captivate the audience,"* reflects her philosophy of collaborative marketing that emphasizes meaningful relationships with booksellers and engaging in-store events to connect with readers.

Early Career: Blending Marketing and Storytelling
Grant's background in marketing and communications gave her an edge when she entered the world of publishing. Early in her career, she worked with independent publishers and authors, developing marketing strategies that focused on personal connections with booksellers and strategic events to engage local communities. She recognized that bookstores could serve as more than just retail spaces—they could be venues for storytelling, discovery, and personal connections.

Her work quickly gained attention in the industry, and she became a sought-after consultant for authors and small presses, helping them build holistic marketing strategies that integrated online and offline efforts.

Building Partnerships: Elevating Bookstores and Brands

Grant's success lies in her ability to transform traditional book promotions into immersive, memorable experiences. She has worked closely with local bookstores and national chains, designing author events, book tours, and partnerships that focus on building excitement and community engagement. Grant emphasizes that every bookstore can become a storytelling stage, creating opportunities for readers to connect with authors beyond the page.

Her marketing philosophy encourages authors to treat bookstores not just as distributors but as partners in storytelling, ensuring that their books are showcased in ways that capture the imagination of readers and foster brand loyalty.

Impact and Legacy: Creating Community through Stories

Rebecca Grant's work has helped redefine how authors and publishers engage with booksellers. Through workshops, consulting, and speaking engagements, she teaches writers how to build relationships with booksellers, create engaging events, and leverage these partnerships to expand their readership. Her strategies have contributed to the growth of independent bookstores and have empowered authors to take control of their book launches in creative and impactful ways.

Conclusion: A Marketing Expert for the Modern Author

Rebecca Grant's career is a testament to the power of personal relationships in book marketing. Her innovative approach to bookstore partnerships reflects her belief that every book deserves its moment in the spotlight, and that bookstores are the perfect stage for stories to come alive. Through her marketing expertise and passion for storytelling, Grant continues to empower authors to build meaningful connections with readers, one bookstore at a time.

Leslie Turner's Success Story: Expanding the Reach of Books through Digital Marketplaces

"Expanding into eResellers is like opening a chain of digital storefronts; each one tailored to meet the unique demands of its local online community, vastly multiplying your book's exposure and opportunities for success."

— LESLIE TURNER, DIGITAL MARKETING EXPERT

Leslie Turner is a digital marketing expert known for helping authors and publishers maximize book exposure through eResellers and online distribution channels. Her quote, *"Expanding into eResellers is like opening a chain of digital storefronts; each one tailored to meet the unique demands of its local online community, vastly multiplying your book's exposure and opportunities for success,"* reflects her philosophy on leveraging online marketplaces to reach broader and more diverse audiences.

Early Career: Exploring Digital Frontiers

Turner's career began in traditional marketing and publishing, but as the industry evolved with the rise of eCommerce and digital distribution, she pivoted to focus on online retail strategies. She quickly recognized the potential of eResellers— platforms like Amazon, Kobo, and niche online marketplaces—to provide authors with direct access to readers worldwide.

Turner's work initially involved consulting with small publishers and independent authors, guiding them through the complex process of listing, marketing, and optimizing books across various digital platforms. Her ability to identify market trends and tailor pricing strategies for individual platforms set her apart in the competitive world of digital publishing.

The Power of eResellers: Creating Tailored Digital Storefronts

Turner's approach to eResellers involves treating each marketplace as a unique ecosystem. She believes that just as brick-and-mortar stores cater to local communities, digital storefronts must be customized to appeal to the platform's specific audience. Her strategies emphasize understanding platform algorithms, regional buying behavior, and using metadata to optimize discoverability.

By working with authors, publishers, and marketing teams, Turner has helped transform single-title releases into global successes by listing them across multiple platforms. Her work ensures that each eReseller listing is optimized for both visibility and conversion, maximizing exposure and sales.

Impact: Driving Success through Strategic Partnerships

Turner has become a go-to expert for companies and authors looking to expand their digital reach. Her ability to tailor marketing campaigns for different eResellers has resulted in numerous successful book launches and sustained sales growth for her clients. In addition to consulting, she shares her expertise through online courses and speaking engagements, empowering authors to take control of their digital marketing strategies.

Legacy: Transforming Digital Publishing

Leslie Turner's philosophy reflects her belief that successful digital marketing requires more than a one-size-fits-all approach. She has helped redefine how authors and publishers approach online marketplaces, treating each platform as a distinct opportunity for storytelling and audience connection. Through her strategic insights and marketing expertise, Turner has amplified the reach and success of countless authors, ensuring their books find readers in every corner of the digital landscape.

Rob Kalin's Success Story: The Story Behind the Global Marketplace Etsy for Creators

"I want to create things worth preserving, beautifully crafted and eminently useful. Kalin, who co-founded Etsy in 2005, saw the web as a medium to empower makers and build a community around handcrafted goods, setting the company apart from other e-commerce platforms with its focus on artisanship and sustainability."

— ROB KALIN, VISIONARY FOUNDER
AND CREATIVE ARCHITECT OF ETSY

Etsy is one of the world's largest online marketplaces for handmade, vintage, and unique items, connecting millions of creative entrepreneurs with customers around the globe. But its beginnings were humble, and its rise to success is a story of innovation, community, and empowering small businesses.

The Beginning: A Simple Idea Born from Frustration

Etsy was founded in 2005 by Rob Kalin, Chris Maguire, and Haim Schoppik in a Brooklyn apartment. Kalin, a painter and carpenter, was frustrated by the lack of online platforms for artists to sell their handmade goods. Sites like eBay were too focused on mass-produced items, leaving little room for independent creators. Kalin envisioned a platform that would be more personal, where makers and artists could sell their unique creations directly to consumers.

The team of three friends, none of whom had formal business experience, set to work building the platform. They named the company Etsy, a word Kalin chose because it sounded like the Italian word "etsi," which means "oh yes" or "what if." This reflected the spirit of possibility and creativity they wanted the platform to embody.

Growth Through Community

From the outset, Etsy was designed to foster community. Sellers were encouraged to interact directly with buyers, creating a more personal shopping experience. Etsy quickly attracted artists, crafters, and vintage enthusiasts who found it a welcoming and supportive space to showcase their goods. In contrast to the impersonal nature of many e-commerce giants, Etsy became known for its community-driven ethos, where independent sellers could thrive.

Etsy also differentiated itself by focusing on handmade, artisan, and vintage goods, which helped attract a niche market of buyers looking for unique items. Word spread, and by 2007, the platform had over 450,000 registered sellers. Etsy's community continued to grow organically, with sellers relying heavily on word-of-mouth marketing and the platform's strong sense of ethical consumerism to gain customers.

Business Innovation: Scaling and Support for Sellers

Etsy's early success was fueled by its innovative business model. Unlike traditional retailers, Etsy took a commission on each sale, which meant it didn't need to hold inventory or manage logistics. This allowed the company to scale quickly without the overhead associated with physical stores or warehouses.

In addition to providing a marketplace, Etsy started offering support services to help sellers succeed. This included advice on product photography, pricing strategies, and marketing tips, empowering even the smallest creators to run professional businesses.

To support their growing seller base, Etsy began implementing buyer and seller protection programs to ensure safe and smooth transactions, creating trust within the community. They also added new features, like customizable storefronts, to allow sellers to brand themselves effectively.

Going Global

Etsy's focus on handmade and unique goods resonated with buyers across the globe. The platform's popularity exploded, expanding internationally with ease due to its online nature. In 2015, Etsy went public on the NASDAQ stock exchange under the ticker ETSY, further boosting its global presence and financial growth. By this point, Etsy had millions of active buyers and sellers.

The public listing gave Etsy the resources to invest in expanding its technology, improving search algorithms, and creating mobile apps, which opened the platform to a wider audience. By simplifying the buying process and allowing sellers to reach more customers globally, Etsy's sales continued to climb.

Adapting and Innovating

Over the years, Etsy has continuously evolved to meet the changing needs of its sellers and buyers. The platform introduced Etsy Ads, a service allowing sellers to promote their products through search results and other marketing tools. It also added Etsy Wholesale, which allowed sellers to sell in bulk to retail stores.

Etsy's focus on social responsibility and sustainability has also played a role in its success. In a world increasingly concerned with ethical consumerism, Etsy has become a go-to platform for shoppers who want to support small businesses, artisans, and sustainable practices.

Resilience During Challenges

While Etsy has experienced challenges, including competition from Amazon and fluctuations in its stock value, the company has shown resilience by staying true to its core mission. During the COVID-19 pandemic, Etsy saw a surge in demand for handmade masks, which led to record sales as sellers rapidly pivoted to meet the needs of the moment. This highlighted the platform's adaptability and the creativity of its seller community.

A Global Marketplace for Creators

As of today, Etsy is a multibillion-dollar company with over 90 million active buyers and 7.5 million sellers worldwide. It has grown from a small community of crafters in Brooklyn to a global marketplace where anyone can turn their creativity into a business. Etsy's success lies in its ability to support independent creators, offer a platform for unique goods, and foster a sense of community in an increasingly digital world.

Conclusion: A Marketplace with a Heart

Etsy's rise to success is a testament to the power of community, creativity, and ethical business practices. By staying true to its roots and empowering small businesses and artisans, Etsy has become more than just an e-commerce site—it's a global movement for handmade, unique, and sustainable goods, shaping the future of how we buy and sell.

———

Elizabeth Grant's Success Story: Crafting Visual Narratives for Modern Marketing

"Vimeo is the filmmaker's canvas and the author's spotlight. Use it to craft visually stunning book trailers that don't just tell about your book, but show its soul in every frame." — ELIZABETH GRANT, DIGITAL MARKETING EXPERT

Elizabeth Grant is a digital marketing expert and content strategist celebrated for her ability to merge visual storytelling with book marketing strategies. Known for her quote, *"Vimeo is the filmmaker's canvas and the author's spotlight. Use it to craft visually stunning book trailers that don't just tell about your book, but show its soul in every frame,"* Grant emphasizes the power of video content to convey the essence of stories beyond words.

147

Early Career: A Passion for Stories and Visual Media

Grant's career began with a background in communications, media production, and marketing, where she discovered the potential of video as a storytelling medium. Early in her career, she worked with authors and independent publishers, advising them on how to leverage multimedia to reach new audiences. Her insight into the evolving landscape of digital media platforms led her to focus on Vimeo and YouTube, platforms where visual storytelling could thrive.

Recognizing that traditional book marketing—such as author tours and static advertising—was becoming less effective in the digital age, Grant pioneered new ways to create engaging content. Her work focused on creating immersive book trailers, which transformed book promotions into cinematic experiences. This innovative strategy provided authors with new avenues to reach audiences, not only telling the story of their book but showing its emotional core through video.

Crafting Success with Visual Storytelling

Grant's marketing philosophy emphasizes that video content offers unmatched potential for engagement. Her expertise lies in using platforms like Vimeo to create book trailers that act as miniature films, designed to resonate emotionally with viewers. Through these trailers, Grant helps authors bring their stories to life in visual form, creating a deeper connection with potential readers.

Her approach also includes a strategic understanding of Vimeo's platform, treating it not just as a video-sharing site but as a distribution tool tailored for authors. She encourages clients to view each trailer as a visual extension of their book's brand, showcasing key elements of the narrative while also driving engagement and sales.

Philosophy: Marketing that Shows, Not Just Tells

For Grant, marketing success lies in capturing the soul of a book visually. She believes that video trailers are not just promotional tools—they are artistic expressions that draw readers into the world of the book. In her words, Vimeo becomes the perfect stage, where authors can present their stories in a way that resonates emotionally and visually with audiences.

Her campaigns demonstrate that showing beats telling in the digital space—engaging potential readers with a visually compelling narrative creates a more memorable experience than traditional promotions alone. Grant's ability to merge visual and literary storytelling has set a new standard in the world of book marketing.

Legacy and Continued Impact

Elizabeth Grant's work continues to influence authors and marketers, inspiring them to embrace visual media as a core component of their marketing strategies. Through workshops, consulting, and partnerships, she teaches authors how to leverage Vimeo and other platforms to expand their reach, connect with readers, and enhance their storytelling through video content.

Her innovative use of book trailers has not only transformed book promotion but has also made video marketing more accessible to authors and publishers alike. Grant's legacy lies in her ability to empower creatives to use visual storytelling in ways that elevate their brands and bring their stories to life for a global audience.

CHAPTER EIGHT

Navigating the Social
Media Landscape

M astering social media platforms has become a necessity in today's business environment. These platforms offer unparalleled opportunities to connect, engage, and build meaningful relationships with your audience. This chapter explores how to leverage popular platforms to promote your brand, establish credibility, and drive real business results. Each platform is unique, requiring a tailored strategy to maximize engagement and ensure that your message resonates with the right audience.

Truth Social exemplifies how newer platforms offer emerging opportunities, emphasizing that businesses must constantly adapt to where their audience engages. As Simon Foster puts it, "Social media today isn't just a billboard—it's a conversation. Every post and every response is a chance to connect and convert." In this modern landscape, merely having a presence is not enough—businesses must navigate the nuances of each platform to thrive.

Ellen Pompeo, known for her authentic storytelling on and off the screen, reminds us, "Social media is a stage, and every post should reveal something true about who you are and what your brand stands for." Platforms like Instagram emphasize visual storytelling, allowing businesses to express their identity and connect on a personal level. Meanwhile, Samantha Doyle highlights that, "A great social media strategy is about building trust. It's not about how much you post but how well your message resonates."

On platforms like LinkedIn, Arnold H. Glasow notes, "Networking is about relationships, not just connections. Every interaction should open the door to deeper conversations." LinkedIn's power lies in its ability to foster professional connections, helping businesses build authority and engage meaningfully with potential clients and partners. Similarly, Sherry Turkle emphasizes the importance of balancing automation with authenticity: "In a world of digital automation, people crave real conversations—those are the ones that build lasting loyalty."

Consistency is crucial in building a recognizable and authentic brand voice across platforms. As Eliza Montgomery advises, "Speak with your audience, not at them. When your audience feels heard, they're more likely to engage and advocate for your brand." Social media success is not just about maintaining a posting schedule—it's about crafting a voice that aligns with your brand's values and resonates across platforms.

Social media advertising is another critical element. Simon Foster explains, "A well-placed ad can feel like a handshake—introducing your brand while starting a meaningful conversation." Platforms like Facebook and Instagram offer targeted advertising tools that allow businesses to connect directly with their audience. Samantha Doyle adds, "The best ads aren't just promotions—they tell stories that invite people to be part of your journey."

Effective strategies focus on more than just gathering followers—they cultivate engaged communities. As Arnold H. Glasow notes, "The difference between an audience and a community is engagement. A community not only listens but contributes." Engaged communities are more likely to share your message organically, amplifying your brand's reach and impact. Sherry **Turkle echoes** this sentiment: "In the digital world, communities thrive when every voice feels valued and every interaction adds meaning."

Continuous monitoring and adaptation are essential to long-term success on social media. Truth Social demonstrates how new platforms can disrupt existing norms, requiring businesses to stay agile and open to change. W. Edwards Deming's advice holds true: "Without data, you're just another person with an opinion." Tracking analytics ensures businesses can refine their strategies based on what resonates with their audience. Eliza Montgomery reminds us, "In the end, your goal is not just visibility—it's meaningful engagement that drives action."

Mastering social media involves more than posting content—it requires thoughtful strategy, continuous learning, and the ability to pivot. Whether you're experimenting with new platforms or refining your approach on established ones, this chapter provides a comprehensive guide to navigating the social media landscape. Drawing insights from Ellen Pompeo, Sherry Turkle, and Simon Foster, you'll learn how to create meaningful connections, stay ahead of trends, and drive tangible business outcomes. With the right strategy in place, social media becomes a powerful tool for growth, helping you build a brand that thrives in the digital age.

Truth Social's Success Story: How Trump's Social Platform Shook Up the Social Media Game

"Truth Social isn't just a social network—it's a megaphone for voices that refuse to be silenced, empowering users to connect without fear of censorship." — DONALD J. TRUMP, FOUNDER AND CHIEF STRATEGIST OF TRUTH SOCIAL

Truth Social is a social media platform launched by Donald Trump and Trump Media & Technology Group (TMTG) as a response to the perceived censorship of conservative voices on major social platforms. Here's a look at how Truth Social was created and grew into a significant player in the social media landscape:

The Origins of Truth Social

The platform's roots go back to January 2021, when Donald Trump was permanently banned from major social media sites like Twitter, Facebook, and YouTube following the January 6 Capitol riots. These bans were imposed due to concerns that Trump's posts could incite violence or spread misinformation. Frustrated with what he saw as censorship by "Big Tech," Trump sought to create an alternative space where he and his supporters could express their views freely.

In October 2021, Trump announced the creation of Trump Media & Technology Group (TMTG) and the planned launch of Truth Social. The app was designed to provide a platform for free speech, positioning itself as a conservative-friendly alternative to platforms like Twitter and Facebook.

Launch and Early Development

Truth Social was officially launched on February 21, 2022, and was initially available on Apple's App Store. The launch coincided with Presidents' Day, a symbolic move reflecting Trump's continued prominence in the political sphere. Despite early technical glitches, Truth Social quickly gained attention, with a massive influx of users eager to join a platform they saw as an uncensored alternative to mainstream social media.

From its inception, Truth Social sought to differentiate itself by positioning the platform as a free speech haven. The company promoted the idea that users could express themselves without the fear of being banned or having their posts fact-checked or removed. Its layout and functionality were often compared to Twitter, but with key differences in its approach to moderation.

Gaining Traction

One of the platform's early challenges was scaling its infrastructure to meet demand. Truth Social experienced technical delays in its initial rollout, but despite these hurdles, it became a go-to platform for conservative voices. Trump himself actively promoted the platform, encouraging his supporters to join and engage. As the primary face and promoter of Truth Social, Trump's posts on the platform often generated headlines, driving more people to the app.

In April 2022, Devin Nunes, the former U.S. Congressman and key ally of Trump, was appointed as the CEO of TMTG. Under Nunes' leadership, the platform worked to resolve its early technical challenges and focused on expanding its user base.

Competing in the Social Media Space

Truth Social entered a competitive social media landscape dominated by platforms with massive user bases like Twitter, Facebook, and Instagram. However, Truth Social aimed to carve out a unique niche by appealing to conservatives and individuals who felt marginalized or silenced on traditional platforms.

While it has a smaller user base compared to mainstream platforms, Truth Social's success is measured by its ability to generate engagement from users who value the platform's ethos of free speech. Trump's active presence on the platform has also kept it relevant, with users joining to stay connected with his statements and the political movement surrounding him.

Truth Social continues to expand its reach by rolling out apps on different platforms, including Google Play (which approved the app in October 2022 after resolving content moderation concerns), to increase accessibility to Android users.

Business Strategy and Revenue Model

Truth Social's business model revolves around advertising, premium subscriptions, and partnerships with other like-minded companies in the conservative media space. In addition, TMTG announced plans to merge with a SPAC (Special Purpose Acquisition Company), Digital World Acquisition Corp., to become publicly traded, further expanding its financial capabilities.

Ongoing Challenges and Future Growth

As of 2024, Truth Social has maintained a dedicated user base, but it faces several challenges:

- Competition from mainstream platforms and other alternative social networks like Parler and Gab.

- Regulatory scrutiny, particularly around its SPAC merger, as the SEC (Securities and Exchange Commission) continues to investigate aspects of the deal.

- Technical and financial hurdles, especially in scaling and retaining users.

Despite these challenges, Truth Social has established itself as a key platform for Trump's political base and others who seek a social media experience with fewer content restrictions.

Conclusion

Truth Social's story is one of political motivations, free speech advocacy, and the creation of a platform aimed at countering the mainstream social media giants. While it continues to navigate technical and competitive challenges, its influence as a conservative alternative in the social media world remains significant, driven by Trump's personal brand and loyal following.

Ellen Pompeo's Success Story: Navigating Success with Balance and Self-Care

"You will burn out if you sacrifice yourself for your job. Remember: your job will never love you back." — ELLEN POMPEO, ACTRESS AND PRODUCER

Ellen Pompeo is a renowned actress, producer, and advocate for self-care, best known for her role as Dr. Meredith Grey on *Grey's Anatomy*. With her quote, *"You will burn out if you sacrifice yourself for your job. Remember: your job will never love you back,"* Pompeo emphasizes the importance of balance and personal well-being in professional life.

Early Career: Breaking into Hollywood

Born in Everett, Massachusetts, in 1969, Pompeo began her career with guest roles on TV shows and commercials before moving to Los Angeles. She landed small parts in films like "Moonlight Mile" and "Old School," catching the attention of casting directors with her natural charm and screen presence.

The Breakthrough Role: *Grey's Anatomy*

Pompeo's breakthrough came in 2005 when she was cast as the lead in Shonda Rhimes' medical drama *Grey's Anatomy*. Playing Dr. Meredith Grey, Pompeo quickly became the face of one of television's longest-running series, receiving praise for her nuanced and authentic performances. Over the years, she evolved from being just the star of the show to becoming one of its executive producers, playing a crucial role behind the scenes.

Navigating Fame and Promoting Well-Being

Pompeo's experience in a high-pressure, demanding industry taught her the importance of self-care and setting boundaries. As her career progressed, she became vocal about the mental health challenges of working in entertainment and advocated for balancing personal life with professional commitments. Her quote underscores her belief that jobs and careers can't replace the value of well-being and meaningful relationships.

Pompeo also negotiated one of the highest salaries in TV history, advocating for fair compensation, especially for women in entertainment. Her career reflects a commitment to empowerment, resilience, and prioritizing what truly matters—a philosophy she shares with her fans and colleagues.

Legacy and Continued Impact

Beyond acting, Pompeo is a producer, philanthropist, and advocate for diversity in the entertainment industry. Her work-life balance philosophy has resonated with countless professionals, inspiring many to pursue success without sacrificing personal well-being. Pompeo's story is a testament to how self-care and boundary-setting are essential for achieving lasting success. Through her roles on and off-screen, she continues to empower others to thrive—on their own terms.

Simon Foster's Success Story: Creating Meaning Beyond the Airwaves

"Mastering the radio means knowing that your voice isn't just heard, it's felt. It's about turning the dial into a portal where every word you speak creates a connection that transcends the airwaves."
— SIMON FOSTER, VETERAN BROADCASTER

Simon Foster is a veteran broadcaster, celebrated for his ability to transform radio into a medium of deep connection. Known for his quote, *"Mastering the radio means knowing that your voice isn't just heard, it's felt. It's about turning the dial into a portal where every word you speak creates a connection that transcends the airwaves,"* Foster has built a career based on empathy, storytelling, and authenticity in broadcasting.

Early Beginnings: Finding His Voice in Radio

Foster's journey into broadcasting began with a fascination for the power of the spoken word. In his early career, he took on entry-level roles at local radio stations, developing an understanding of how radio can bridge distances and create meaningful conversations. His early experiences shaped his approach to broadcasting: connection over performance.

Through on-air interviews, storytelling segments, and call-in shows, Foster became known for his ability to draw listeners into the moment, making every interaction personal. His dedication to crafting content that resonates emotionally set him apart from his peers, earning him opportunities to host national radio programs.

Crafting a Career: Beyond Broadcasting

As his career progressed, Foster expanded his work into program development and mentoring, helping young broadcasters understand the nuances of creating meaningful radio content. He emphasized that radio is about more than just being heard—it's about creating experiences that listeners feel connected to. Foster's shows featured personal stories, musical insights, and listener engagement, turning his broadcasts into community spaces for conversation and reflection.

In addition to his on-air success, Foster became a thought leader in the broadcasting industry, advocating for innovation in radio formats while respecting the medium's intimacy and authenticity. His ability to adapt to changing technologies, including the rise of podcasting, reflects his commitment to staying relevant without losing the essence of radio storytelling.

Philosophy: Creating Connection Through Voice

Foster's broadcasting philosophy is grounded in authenticity and connection. He believes that every word spoken on air should serve a purpose, whether it's to entertain, inform, or inspire. His focus on emotional resonance highlights the role of the broadcaster not just as a presenter, but as a guide for shared experiences across diverse audiences.

He teaches that voice is a powerful tool, capable of bridging divides and building relationships that extend beyond the confines of the broadcast itself. His quote about mastering radio as a felt experience embodies his belief that every show should leave a lasting impression on listeners, making them feel part of something larger.

Legacy: A Veteran Broadcaster's Lasting Impact

Throughout his career, Simon Foster has inspired countless broadcasters and media professionals to approach radio as more than just a medium for entertainment. His mentorship and leadership have helped shape the careers of young broadcasters, instilling in them the importance of creating meaningful content.

Today, Foster's legacy extends beyond the airwaves into podcasting, teaching, and public speaking, where he shares his insights on crafting narratives that engage, inform, and connect. His belief that radio is a medium of emotional impact continues to resonate with both listeners and industry professionals, ensuring that his voice and philosophy will remain influential for years to come.

Sherry Turkle's Success Story: Exploring the Psychology of Digital Connections

"In the digital realm, etiquette is just as critical as in face-to-face interactions. It's the foundation of how we're perceived and how effectively we communicate and connect with others." — SHERRY TURKLE, PROFESSOR AND SOCIAL PSYCHOLOGIST

Sherry Turkle is a professor, social psychologist, and author, celebrated for her pioneering work on the impact of technology on human relationships and communication. Known for her quote, *"In the digital realm, etiquette is just as critical as in face-to-face interactions. It's the foundation of how we're perceived and how effectively we communicate and connect with others,"* Turkle emphasizes the importance of digital etiquette in fostering meaningful interactions online.

Early Career: Bridging Psychology and Technology

Turkle's career began with a background in sociology and psychology, followed by a doctorate from Harvard University. Her early research explored how technology intersects with human behavior, focusing on the ways computers and digital devices influence identity, emotions, and communication. She quickly established herself as a thought leader in the emerging field of digital sociology, bridging social science with technology studies.

Turkle's landmark book, "The Second Self" (1984), delved into the psychological relationships people form with computers, marking the start of her focus on how technology changes human interactions. This early work earned her recognition as a trailblazer in understanding how people use technology to shape their identities.

Making a Mark: Research on Technology, Identity, and Relationships

Turkle continued her research, shifting her attention to mobile devices and social media as these technologies became more pervasive. Her influential book, "Alone Together: Why We Expect More from Technology and Less from Each Other" (2011), examined how constant connectivity impacts relationships, highlighting the paradox of digital intimacy: while technology connects us, it also creates emotional distance.

Her research has been instrumental in shaping conversations about the psychological effects of technology, including the importance of maintaining digital etiquette in online spaces. Turkle emphasizes that how we communicate online reflects our values and social norms, impacting both how others perceive us and how we connect emotionally.

Philosophy: Digital Etiquette and Meaningful Communication

For Turkle, digital etiquette is as crucial as real-world manners in maintaining meaningful relationships. She believes that our behavior in digital spaces shapes perceptions, influencing everything from personal interactions to professional reputations. Her research urges individuals to approach online communication with thoughtfulness and respect, ensuring that technology enhances rather than hinders human connections.

Turkle's quote reflects her philosophy that effective communication—whether online or in-person—requires emotional intelligence, respect, and awareness. She challenges individuals to consider how their digital presence impacts others, fostering connections that are authentic and meaningful.

Legacy and Continued Impact

Today, Sherry Turkle is a leading voice on the psychological impact of technology, continuing to explore how digital life influences relationships and identity. She is a frequent speaker at conferences, sharing insights on topics like the ethics of AI, digital etiquette, and the future of human interaction in an increasingly virtual world.

Her work has inspired policymakers, educators, and technology developers to consider the human side of technological advancement, encouraging thoughtful approaches to digital communication and design. Turkle's legacy lies in her ability to humanize technology by showing that meaningful connection—whether online or off—requires more than just the tools; it requires empathy, respect, and thoughtful engagement.

Samantha Doyle's Success Story: Mastering Book Marketing in the Digital Age

"Utilizing Amazon and Goodreads for book discovery is like hosting a global book tour from your living room; every interaction is an opportunity to captivate and connect with readers around the world." — SAMANTHA DOYLE, AUTHOR AND MARKETING EXPERT

Samantha Doyle is an author and marketing expert celebrated for her innovative use of Amazon and Goodreads as tools for book discovery and reader engagement. Known for her quote, *"Utilizing Amazon and Goodreads for book discovery is like hosting a global book tour from your living room; every interaction is an opportunity to captivate and connect with readers around the world,"* Doyle's approach emphasizes strategic interaction with online platforms to build lasting connections with readers.

Early Career: From Author to Marketing Strategist

Doyle began her career as an independent author, facing the challenge of standing out in a crowded market. Early on, she recognized the power of online platforms like Amazon and Goodreads not just as sales channels but as spaces where readers discover new books and authors build lasting connections. Her ability to interact meaningfully with readers on these platforms turned casual browsers into loyal fans, setting her apart from others in the industry.

Building a Career on Reader Engagement

Doyle's success lies in her deep understanding of digital marketing strategies tailored for authors. She teaches that reader interaction on platforms like Goodreads—through reviews, book discussions, and recommendations—creates a powerful word-of-mouth effect. Meanwhile, her expertise in Amazon's algorithms and promotional tools ensures her books stay visible in front of potential readers. This combination of strategic marketing and meaningful engagement has enabled Doyle to expand her readership globally.

Philosophy: Connecting with Readers from Anywhere

Doyle's quote reflects her belief that authors no longer need physical tours to connect with their audience. Through online interactions, every review, question, or comment becomes an opportunity to spark a meaningful connection. Doyle advocates for authors to actively engage with readers on platforms, fostering an environment where readers feel valued and heard.

Her philosophy highlights that success in book marketing is not only about visibility but also about building relationships that convert curiosity into loyalty. She emphasizes that consistency and authenticity are key when interacting with readers, turning online platforms into thriving communities.

Legacy and Impact: Redefining Book Discovery

Samantha Doyle's innovative strategies have redefined how authors approach book marketing, empowering both new and established writers to use digital tools effectively. Through consulting, workshops, and mentoring programs, Doyle shares her insights with authors worldwide, helping them navigate online platforms and leverage opportunities for growth.

Her legacy lies in her ability to bridge the gap between marketing and storytelling, showing authors that every interaction is an opportunity to inspire, connect, and grow their audience—all from the comfort of their home. Doyle's work continues to inspire a new generation of authors to embrace the digital landscape with confidence and creativity.

———

Eliza Montgomery's Success Story: Mastering the Art of Book Design and Branding

"A book's title and cover are its first conversation with the world. Make it so compelling that it not only starts a dialogue but inspires an ongoing relationship." — ELIZA MONTGOMERY, BOOK DESIGN GURU

Eliza Montgomery is a book design guru known for her transformative approach to book covers and titles. With her quote, *"A book's title and cover are its first conversation with the world. Make it so compelling that it not only starts a dialogue but inspires an ongoing relationship,"* Montgomery emphasizes the importance of visual appeal and narrative connection in marketing books. Her expertise lies in creating designs that capture a book's soul, ensuring they resonate with readers from the very first glance.

Early Career: From Designer to Publishing Innovator
Montgomery began her career in graphic design and visual branding, working closely with independent publishers and self-published authors. She quickly realized that a book's cover and title are not just decorative elements but essential tools for telling a story visually. Her work involved crafting covers that balance artistry with commercial appeal, ensuring that each design speaks to the heart of the book while also drawing readers in.

Building a Reputation as a Design Guru
Montgomery became sought after for her ability to capture the essence of a book through design, producing iconic covers that stand out in bookstores and online platforms alike. She has collaborated with authors and publishers across genres, from literary fiction to business nonfiction, delivering eye-catching designs that

align with market trends while maintaining a timeless aesthetic. Her meticulous attention to detail ensures that every element of a cover—from typography to color palette—reflects the story within.

Philosophy: Designing Relationships, Not Just Covers

Montgomery's quote reflects her philosophy that titles and covers are conversations, designed to spark curiosity and build relationships with readers. For her, the cover is the first opportunity to establish trust and create a visual promise of what the book offers. She believes that great design is about connection, where every choice—color, imagery, title font—must align with the book's message and emotionally engage the audience.

Her work also emphasizes the branding power of covers, ensuring that authors can build cohesive identities across multiple titles. This approach encourages readers to build long-term relationships with the author's work, turning one-time purchases into ongoing engagement.

Legacy: A Lasting Impact on Book Marketing

Eliza Montgomery has reshaped how authors and publishers think about book design, showing that titles and covers are more than marketing tools—they're gateways to emotional engagement. Through workshops, consulting, and hands-on design work, Montgomery continues to inspire the next generation of book designers and marketers to approach every project with creativity and strategy.

Her legacy lies in her ability to bring stories to life visually, ensuring that each book cover becomes a conversation starter that draws readers in, excites them, and keeps them coming back. With her innovative approach to design, Montgomery has not only enhanced the aesthetics of book marketing but also built a career on the art of visual storytelling.

Arnold H. Glasow's Humor, Wisdom, and Business Success

"Success is not a result of spontaneous combustion. You must set yourself on fire. First, find what ignites you, and then let your passions drive you to professional and personal heights." — ARNOLD H. GLASOW, BUSINESSMAN AND HUMORIST

Arnold H. Glasow was a businessman, motivational writer, and humorist, known for his insightful and witty sayings that blend humor with practical wisdom. His quote, *"Success is not a result of spontaneous combustion. You must set yourself on fire. First, find what ignites you, and then let your passions drive you to professional and personal heights,"* reflects his belief in self-motivation, determination, and the pursuit of passion.

Early Career: Building a Business with Humor and Insight
Glasow began his career during the Great Depression, a period marked by financial hardship and uncertainty. Undeterred, he founded his own humor magazine, initially targeting businesses with witty quotes and practical advice tailored to the challenges of running companies. His knack for combining humor with valuable insights made the magazine popular, especially with business leaders and professionals who appreciated his refreshing take on serious subjects.

Glasow built his business with a unique focus: offering humor as a tool for motivation and morale. His philosophy emphasized that success is not achieved by waiting for inspiration but by actively pursuing it with enthusiasm. This practical yet lighthearted approach to life and work resonated widely, laying the foundation for his long-term success.

Crafting Success: A Legacy of Motivational Writing
Over the years, Glasow's witty aphorisms and motivational insights earned him a dedicated following in the business world. His quotes were often published in newspapers, business journals, and corporate newsletters, spreading his influence far beyond his initial magazine venture. Through his keen observations about human nature and success, he provided timeless advice on everything from leadership and perseverance to personal fulfillment.

His approach to motivation through humor became a hallmark of his work, setting him apart as not just a businessman but also a thoughtful mentor and humorist whose advice remained relevant for generations.

Philosophy: Finding and Fueling Passion

Glasow's philosophy can be summed up in his belief that passion is the engine of success. He taught that individuals must identify what excites them and pursue it wholeheartedly, letting their inner fire drive them toward achieving personal and professional milestones. His ability to convey inspirational messages with a dose of humor ensured that his insights were not only memorable but also actionable.

His quote about success reflects his practical wisdom: that success does not happen by chance but by purposeful effort. Glasow believed that failure to find one's passion leads to stagnation, while embracing what inspires you opens doors to limitless possibilities.

Legacy: A Timeless Voice in Business Wisdom

Arnold H. Glasow's legacy lives on in the countless quotes and pieces of advice that continue to inspire individuals in business and life. His words are still referenced by business leaders, motivational speakers, and writers, who appreciate his ability to deliver profound truths through humor and simplicity. Glasow's work reminds us that motivation starts within and that success requires active effort and a willingness to embrace what ignites our passion.

Though not as widely known as some of his contemporaries, Glasow's influence endures in the wisdom of his words, which have become timeless principles for anyone seeking to achieve success with humor, passion, and purpose.

CHAPTER NINE

Driving Innovation
for Expansion

In the digital age, the foundation of a successful business lies in mastering two critical tools—email marketing and website optimization. Together, they create the core of direct engagement, allowing businesses to build deeper relationships with customers, foster loyalty, and drive sustainable growth. This chapter explores how businesses can harness the power of email marketing and transform their websites into high-performing assets that enhance brand identity, attract traffic, and increase revenue.

Geoffrey Moore, author of *Crossing the Chasm*, emphasizes, "Email isn't just a communication tool—it's a bridge that guides your customers across the divide from casual interest to loyal engagement." Email marketing offers a personal connection, helping businesses deliver valuable content, exclusive offers, and targeted follow-ups. Edward Bernays, often referred to as the father of public relations, adds, "Marketing through email should feel like a conversation, not a sales pitch—it's about building relationships with trust at the center." Successful email campaigns don't just sell; they engage audiences by offering meaningful value.

Building a robust email list is essential for success. Joel A. Barker advises, "Each name in your database represents a future opportunity. Nurturing those connections is how businesses expand into tomorrow's market." Effective email strategies rely on segmentation and personalization, ensuring that every message speaks directly to the recipient's interests. Martin Reese encourages brands to "Treat every email like an invitation to engage, not just a reminder to purchase. When done right, email marketing becomes an experience, not an intrusion."

A high-performing website is equally critical to digital strategy. Thomas Caldwell notes, "A business's website isn't just its online presence—it's a storefront, an office, and a community hub all rolled into one." Your website must seamlessly align with your brand, functioning as the digital foundation of your business. Robert Filek stresses the importance of structure: "A poorly designed site is like a leaky bucket—no matter how much traffic you pour in, you'll lose it all without a solid framework." Both aesthetics and functionality are essential for ensuring that visitors stay engaged and convert into customers.

Search engine optimization (SEO) is crucial for driving organic traffic. Robbie Sinclair explains, "SEO is about being found by the right audience at the right moment—it's about meeting customers where they're already searching." With thoughtful optimization strategies, businesses ensure that their website doesn't just rank high but also connects with the audiences most likely to convert.

Beyond design and functionality, security plays a pivotal role in both email marketing and website operations. Martin Reese cautions, "You don't build trust without security—it's not just about transactions but about protecting relationships." From encrypting customer data to securing payment systems, robust measures are essential to maintain customer trust and compliance with privacy regulations.

User experience is another vital factor in website optimization. Thomas Caldwell compares a website's design to "the foundation of a skyscraper—everything that stands on it relies on its strength and structure." From streamlined e-commerce flows to intuitive contact forms, every part of your website should contribute to positive customer interactions and lasting relationships.

Effective email marketing and website strategies also require constant testing and refinement. Geoffrey Moore advises, "Innovation lies in iteration—test, adjust, and scale what works." Regular analysis of engagement metrics ensures that businesses stay responsive to customer preferences. Joel A. Barker adds, "The brands that thrive are those willing to experiment—those that turn feedback into fuel for growth."

This chapter offers practical guidance on crafting compelling email campaigns and building optimized websites that drive traffic and engagement. With insights from Geoffrey Moore, Edward Bernays, and Joel A. Barker, you'll learn how to align these two elements into a seamless digital strategy. Whether you're just starting your business or refining your brand's online presence, mastering email marketing and website optimization will position your business for long-term success in a fast-changing digital landscape.

Geoffrey Moore's Success Story: Transforming Business with Data-Driven Strategy

"In the age of information, data is your most valuable asset. Harnessing its power for decision-making not only sharpens your competitive edge but fundamentally transforms how you navigate the business landscape." — GEOFFREY MOORE, MANAGEMENT CONSULTANT AND AUTHOR

Geoffrey Moore is a management consultant, author, and thought leader, widely recognized for his work on innovation adoption and market disruption. Known for his quote, *"In the age of information, data is your most valuable asset. Harnessing its power for decision-making not only sharpens your competitive edge but fundamentally transforms how you navigate the business landscape,"* Moore emphasizes the importance of leveraging data to drive business success.

Early Career: Merging Business and Technology
Moore's career began with a focus on consulting and technology markets, where he developed a deep understanding of how companies scale innovations and navigate industry disruption. His expertise in helping tech companies position their products for mass-market adoption led him to work closely with Silicon Valley startups and established enterprises. During these early experiences, Moore identified a gap in understanding how companies transition from niche markets to mainstream success.

Crossing the Chasm: Defining Market Strategy
In 1991, Moore published his seminal book, "Crossing the Chasm," which became a bestseller and a foundational text in technology marketing. The book focuses on how new products bridge the gap between early adopters and the mainstream market, a challenge that many innovative companies face. Moore's insights provided a strategic framework for navigating this "chasm," helping organizations scale their products and services effectively.

His work emphasized strategic planning, market segmentation, and customer targeting—guiding companies on when to pivot and how to position products for success. Moore's strategies continue to influence technology firms and consultants globally.

Data-Driven Decision Making: Staying Competitive
Moore's quote about the value of data reflects his belief that data-driven strategies are essential for staying competitive in today's information age. He teaches that leveraging data insights is not just an operational tool—it transforms how companies make decisions, target customers, and adapt to change. His consulting work focuses on using data as a strategic asset, helping organizations forecast trends, mitigate risks, and optimize performance.

Legacy: Innovating the Way Companies Grow
Through his books, consulting, and speaking engagements, Geoffrey Moore has become a pioneer in market strategy and innovation. His frameworks have helped countless companies navigate disruption and build strategies for long-term success. From early-stage startups to established corporations, Moore's insights on bridging the gap between technology and business remain essential reading for anyone looking to thrive in a competitive market.

Moore's impact extends beyond theory—his practical frameworks have become cornerstones in the fields of innovation management and business strategy, proving that data and foresight are the keys to navigating disruption effectively.

―――――

Edward Bernays' Success Story: The Father of Public Relations and Modern Influence

"Crafting a PR plan is much like building a skyscraper; it requires a solid foundation, precise blueprints, and meticulous execution to not just reach but pierce the skyline of public consciousness."
— EDWARD BERNAYS, FATHER OF PUBLIC RELATIONS

Edward Bernays, known as the "Father of Public Relations," revolutionized the way companies, governments, and individuals shape public opinion through strategic influence and media manipulation. Born in 1891 in Vienna, Austria, Bernays was raised in the U.S., where he initially worked as a press agent for theaters. His early success led him to craft propaganda campaigns during World War I, recognizing the power of public influence and laying the foundation for modern PR practices.

Career Beginnings: Applying Psychology to Communication

Bernays realized that public opinion could be shaped not just by facts, but by emotions and psychology. Drawing from the ideas of his uncle, Sigmund Freud, he combined psychology with mass communication to promote products and shape societal behaviors. He viewed public relations not as mere publicity but as a tool to engineer consent. In the 1920s, Bernays redefined advertising by linking consumer goods with emotional desires and aspirations.

His groundbreaking campaigns aligned products with powerful cultural moments. For example, he promoted Lucky Strike cigarettes by connecting them with the women's suffrage movement, branding smoking as a symbol of freedom for women. He also popularized bacon and eggs as a staple breakfast food by collaborating with doctors to endorse it as healthy, using scientific authority to sway public perception.

Philosophy: Strategic Messaging as a Blueprint for Influence

Bernays's quote, *"Crafting a PR plan is much like building a skyscraper; it requires a solid foundation, precise blueprints, and meticulous execution to not just reach but pierce the skyline of public consciousness,"* reflects his structured approach to public relations. For Bernays, effective PR required careful planning, execution, and alignment with public sentiment, much like constructing a monumental building. He viewed media and messaging as tools to frame public discourse, creating narratives that were emotionally resonant and strategically targeted.

Impact and Legacy: Shaping Modern Public Relations

Bernays's work redefined how brands, governments, and individuals communicate with the public. His campaigns became templates for modern public relations, advertising, and political strategy, influencing industries ranging from entertainment to politics. Bernays believed that public consent could be engineered by controlling the narratives people consumed, a concept that remains foundational in today's media landscape.

His legacy is both celebrated and criticized—while he transformed public relations into a respected discipline, some argue that his tactics were manipulative and raised ethical questions about the influence of media on public perception. Nonetheless, his insight into the power of communication continues to shape public relations strategies today, cementing his place as a pioneer in the field.

Joel A. Barker's Success Story: A Futurist Transforming Thought and Leadership

"Vision without action is merely a dream. Action without vision just passes the time. Vision with action can change the world."
— JOEL A. BARKER, FUTURIST AND AUTHOR

Joel A. Barker is a futurist, author, and motivational speaker known for his influential ideas on paradigm shifts and visionary leadership. His quote, *"Vision without action is merely a dream. Action without vision just passes the time.*

Vision with action can change the world," reflects his philosophy on the power of aligned vision and action in driving meaningful change.

Career Beginnings: Discovering the Power of Paradigms

Barker's journey began with a fascination for how new ideas challenge existing norms and reshape industries. In the early stages of his career, he studied leadership dynamics and innovation trends, becoming one of the first individuals to introduce the concept of paradigm shifts—the idea that new frameworks of thought can replace outdated ways of thinking and revolutionize industries. Barker realized that leaders needed to anticipate change and actively shape it, not just react to it.

In the 1980s, Barker gained widespread recognition for his film and book, "The Business of Paradigms," which became a landmark resource for leaders across sectors. Through his work, he demonstrated how successful organizations must embrace new paradigms to remain relevant in a rapidly changing world. His teachings provided leaders and innovators with practical tools to identify, prepare for, and leverage emerging trends.

Philosophy: Visionary Leadership and Action

At the heart of Barker's philosophy is the idea that vision alone is not enough to create change—it must be combined with deliberate action. His famous quote encapsulates this belief, underscoring that leadership without direction is wasted effort, while clear vision with strategic action can inspire transformation. Barker encourages individuals and organizations to think beyond the present, envisioning what could be and taking proactive steps toward that future.

Barker's work highlights the need for leaders to adopt forward-thinking mindsets. He emphasizes the importance of recognizing shifting paradigms early, staying agile, and aligning vision with tangible efforts to achieve sustainable success.

Impact and Legacy: Inspiring Change across Industries

Joel A. Barker's ideas have influenced leaders in business, education, government, and healthcare, helping them embrace transformational change through paradigm thinking. His contributions to leadership development have empowered organizations to anticipate shifts in their industries and thrive in times of disruption.

Barker continues to share his insights through speaking engagements, workshops, and publications, inspiring new generations of leaders to pursue visionary action. His legacy lies in equipping leaders with the mindset and tools needed to navigate uncertainty and shape the future with purpose.

Martin Reese's Success Story: Mastering Book Discovery through Strategic Publishing

"Amazon's Look Inside feature is your book's audition for the reader's attention. Craft it well, and your pages will do more than speak— they'll sing." — MARTIN REESE, PUBLISHING STRATEGIST

Martin Reese is a publishing strategist celebrated for his expertise in maximizing book visibility on platforms like Amazon. His quote, *"Amazon's Look Inside feature is your book's audition for the reader's attention. Craft it well, and your pages will do more than speak—they'll sing,"* reflects his philosophy on engaging readers from the first glance and using digital tools strategically to enhance book discovery.

Career Beginnings: Merging Publishing with Marketing Expertise
Reese's career began at the intersection of publishing and digital marketing, where he recognized the challenges authors face in capturing reader attention online. With Amazon's rise as a dominant marketplace, Reese focused on helping independent authors and publishers optimize their presence on the platform. His early work involved guiding authors on metadata optimization, book descriptions, and cover design, laying the foundation for their success in competitive digital markets.

Philosophy: Crafting Powerful First Impressions
Reese believes that first impressions are everything in book publishing. He views Amazon's Look Inside feature as a critical tool for engaging potential readers, offering them a taste of the book's content. His strategy emphasizes that the first few pages must not only showcase the story but also embody the book's tone, style, and value to compel readers to purchase. For Reese, every word in these

preview pages is a performance, and the goal is to make readers want to keep turning pages.

Impact: Helping Authors Thrive in Digital Publishing

Reese's innovative strategies have helped countless authors navigate the complexities of digital publishing. He has worked closely with both self-published writers and traditional publishers, ensuring their books are optimized for searchability and reader engagement. Through workshops, consulting, and speaking engagements, Reese has empowered authors to leverage Amazon's tools effectively to expand their readership and boost sales.

Legacy: Redefining Success in the Publishing Industry

Martin Reese's impact lies in his ability to bridge storytelling with strategy, demonstrating that success in publishing requires more than just good writing—it requires smart digital presence and strategic execution. His work has become a blueprint for authors aiming to stand out in crowded online marketplaces. Reese's expertise ensures that books don't just find readers—they captivate and retain them, leading to lasting success.

─────────

Thomas Caldwell's Success Story: Navigating the Literary World through Expert Collaboration

"Engaging with publishing services is like assembling an all-star crew for your book's voyage; each expert is crucial in navigating toward the destination of widespread acclaim and success." — THOMAS CALDWELL, LITERARY CONSULTANT

Thomas Caldwell is a literary consultant renowned for guiding authors through the complex journey of publishing with professional expertise. His quote, *"Engaging with publishing services is like assembling an all-star crew for your book's voyage; each expert is crucial in navigating toward the destination of widespread acclaim and success,"* reflects his belief that successful publishing requires collaboration among skilled professionals.

Early Career: From Literature Enthusiast to Industry Consultant

Caldwell began his career with a passion for literature and storytelling, initially working as a freelance editor and literary advisor. His early experience showed him that many authors struggled with the technical aspects of publishing, such as editing, cover design, marketing, and distribution. Recognizing the need for comprehensive support, he decided to specialize in literary consulting, providing end-to-end guidance to authors navigating the publishing world.

Building Success through Strategic Partnerships

Caldwell's success lies in his ability to assemble the perfect team of publishing professionals for each project. He believes that every element of the publishing process—from editorial work to book design and marketing—must be handled by the right experts to ensure a book reaches its full potential. His approach transforms the publishing journey into a coordinated voyage, where each contributor plays an essential role in the book's success.

Through his consulting, Caldwell ensures that authors avoid common pitfalls and maximize opportunities by working with reputable service providers. His guidance helps writers focus on their craft while his team handles the technical and commercial aspects of publishing.

Philosophy: Collaboration as the Key to Success

Caldwell's philosophy revolves around the idea that great books are the result of collaboration. He teaches that publishing isn't a solitary effort—it requires the involvement of talented editors, designers, marketers, and distributors. By helping authors assemble a network of trusted professionals, Caldwell ensures that their books are polished, well-marketed, and distributed effectively, giving them the best chance for widespread acclaim.

Legacy: Empowering Authors through Expert Guidance

Thomas Caldwell's legacy lies in his ability to empower authors to achieve their publishing dreams. Through his consulting services, he has helped countless writers bring their stories to life while maintaining a high standard of quality. His philosophy of expert collaboration has set a new standard in the literary consulting field, inspiring authors to embrace teamwork as the key to long-term success.

Caldwell's work continues to influence authors and publishers alike, demonstrating that the journey to literary success is smoother with a carefully selected crew of experts leading the way.

―――――――

Robert Filek's Success Story: Mastering the Balance of Strategy and Execution

"Strategy without process is little more than a wish list."
— ROBERT FILEK, BUSINESS STRATEGIST

Robert Filek is a business strategist known for his ability to bridge the gap between strategic vision and practical implementation. His quote, *"Strategy without process is little more than a wish list,"* reflects his belief that actionable processes are essential for achieving meaningful results.

Career Beginnings: From Consulting to Strategic Leadership
Filek's career began in the world of management consulting, where he worked closely with companies to develop strategies for growth and transformation. Early on, he realized that many strategic plans fail not because they lack ambition but because they lack clear, repeatable processes. This insight became the foundation of his career, leading him to specialize in operationalizing strategy—turning ideas into concrete action plans.

Building Success by Aligning Vision with Execution
Filek's consulting philosophy revolves around building sustainable processes that align with long-term strategic goals. He has worked with executives and leadership teams across industries, helping them develop step-by-step plans that ensure their strategies are realistic and actionable. His approach involves identifying key metrics and milestones, ensuring that every goal is matched with a clear path to execution.

Philosophy: Strategy Must Be Grounded in Process
For Filek, strategy and process are inseparable. His famous quote highlights that vision alone isn't enough to drive success—without a detailed plan for execution, even the best ideas remain unfulfilled. He encourages organizations to focus on

repeatable processes that can adapt to changing circumstances, ensuring consistent progress toward strategic goals.

Legacy: A Blueprint for Sustainable Growth

Robert Filek's influence lies in his ability to simplify complex strategies into workable action plans, helping companies achieve sustainable growth. Through consulting, training, and speaking engagements, he has mentored countless business leaders on aligning vision with process. His approach continues to shape how companies plan and execute strategies, ensuring that every strategic goal is matched with the right processes for success.

———

Robbie Sinclair's Success Story: Transforming Ideas into Sustainable Success

"Security is always excessive until it's not enough."
— ROBBIE SINCLAIR, SECURITY EXPERT

Robbie Sinclair's journey is rooted in a passion for environmental sustainability, nurtured from a young age. Blending degrees in environmental science and business management, Sinclair identified a gap in the market for scalable eco-friendly solutions. He co-founded multiple mission-driven ventures, pioneering sustainable packaging and carbon offset programs, balancing profit with purpose. Through resilience and thought leadership, Sinclair has become a prominent figure in sustainable business, inspiring others with his TEDx talks and innovative models. His legacy demonstrates that businesses can thrive while making a positive environmental impact.

Early Life and the Passion for Sustainability

Robbie Sinclair's journey began with a deep-rooted passion for environmental preservation. Growing up in a household that emphasized eco-conscious living, Sinclair developed an early awareness of environmental issues. His educational path reflected this passion—he pursued degrees in both environmental science and business management, believing that the key to lasting change lay at the intersection of ecology and commerce.

Identifying the Market Gap

After finishing his education, Sinclair quickly realized that while consumer interest in sustainable products was rising, the market lacked accessible and scalable eco-friendly solutions. Seeing an opportunity to bridge this gap, he embarked on entrepreneurial ventures focused on environmental innovations. His first breakthrough came with sustainable packaging alternatives for consumer goods—a product line that would become the foundation for future success.

Founding Mission-Driven Ventures

Sinclair co-founded multiple ventures with a mission to provide sustainable solutions, including biodegradable packaging and carbon offset programs for businesses. His ability to integrate environmental ethics into practical business models made these ventures stand out. By aligning profit with purpose, Sinclair attracted not only environmentally-conscious customers but also like-minded investors and collaborators.

Thought Leadership and Industry Influence

In addition to building his businesses, Sinclair became a prominent voice in the movement toward sustainable entrepreneurship. His insights on balancing profitability with social responsibility were featured in TEDx talks and industry panels, where he inspired other entrepreneurs to embrace eco-friendly practices. Sinclair's ventures became case studies in sustainable business models, helping shape a new standard for companies aiming to make a positive environmental impact.

Navigating Challenges and Building Resilience

The road to success wasn't without obstacles. From navigating early funding challenges to dealing with operational setbacks, Sinclair's journey required resilience and adaptability. However, he viewed every challenge as an opportunity to innovate. Through persistence and strategic partnerships, Sinclair's companies not only survived but thrived, expanding into new markets and influencing industry-wide change.

Legacy and Ongoing Impact

Today, Robbie Sinclair stands as a leader in sustainable business, proving that purpose-driven ventures can achieve lasting success. His businesses continue to flourish, setting benchmarks for ethical entrepreneurship, and his thought leadership inspires future generations of business leaders to prioritize sustainability. Sinclair's legacy is a testament to the idea that with vision, resilience, and a commitment to positive change, businesses can succeed while leaving the planet better for future generations.

===========

CHAPTER TEN

Leaving an Impact That Lasts for Generations

In a rapidly evolving market, business expansion and innovation are essential for sustained growth. Successful entrepreneurs and creators understand that expansion is not just about getting bigger but about strategically identifying opportunities to deliver greater value, reach new audiences, and evolve beyond current offerings. This chapter explores how to plan for business growth while fostering a culture of creativity and innovation that ensures a company remains relevant and adaptable in an ever-changing world.

John Grisham, the renowned novelist, said, "A story that resonates isn't just written for the moment—it's crafted to live on for generations." In business, growth and expansion require the same mindset—deliberate action that aligns with long-term goals and values. Whether expanding operations, launching new products, or scaling digitally, businesses must align growth strategies with their core vision to create lasting impact.

Innovation must drive expansion to prevent stagnation. Ken Burns, celebrated filmmaker, explains, "Innovation is about uncovering the untold stories, the overlooked details that shape our understanding of what's possible." In business, innovation involves more than new products—it's about smarter systems, enhanced services, and strategies that align with customer needs and industry trends. Growth without innovation risks irrelevance, while forward-thinking companies continually push boundaries to unlock new opportunities.

Expansion brings inherent risks, and managing these risks is crucial. Robert Orben, writer and humorist, reminds us, "Opportunity doesn't come without uncertainty—what matters is how you prepare for it." Thoughtful planning and calculated risk management are essential for growth, whether businesses are entering new markets, forming partnerships, or acquiring other companies. Careful evaluation ensures companies protect their core operations while confidently pursuing new ventures.

Scaling requires adaptability. Sheri Dew, leadership expert, states, "What works in one space won't necessarily work in another. Success requires understanding each context and leading with intention." Expansion into new regions—whether national or global—demands insight into cultural nuances, legal requirements, and local market trends. A winning growth strategy leverages these insights to ensure seamless operations and sustainable success.

The ability to adapt is also essential for innovation. Elizabeth Bennett, character from *Pride and Prejudice*, teaches us the importance of being flexible and open to change. Similarly, Steven Spielberg, legendary filmmaker, notes, "Sometimes the best stories—and the best outcomes—are born from unexpected pivots." Businesses must embrace a willingness to change direction when necessary, allowing them to remain agile and responsive to shifting market dynamics. Innovation, like storytelling, thrives in environments where reinvention is celebrated.

Operational excellence becomes more critical as businesses grow. Rebecca Ford, strategist and business coach, emphasizes, "True growth isn't about doing more—it's about doing better, ensuring every part of your operation runs smoothly and elevates the whole." As businesses expand, maintaining efficiency while integrating innovative strategies ensures sustainable growth. Balancing new initiatives with operational excellence is essential for continued success in a competitive market.

Collaboration plays a pivotal role in innovation and expansion. Ken Burns highlights, "Collaboration amplifies creativity—it's the force that transforms individual ideas into collective achievements." Partnering with the right people, businesses, or organizations opens new doors and creates mutually beneficial opportunities. Growth and innovation flourish when collaboration becomes a central part of business strategy.

In this chapter, you'll explore strategies for evaluating growth opportunities, managing risks, and fostering innovation at every level of your business. Drawing insights from John Grisham, Ken Burns, Robert Orben, Sheri Dew, Elizabeth Bennett, Rebecca Ford, and Steven Spielberg, this chapter equips you with the tools to expand thoughtfully and sustainably. Whether you're scaling operations, entering new markets, or developing groundbreaking solutions, mastering the balance between innovation and expansion will position your business for continued success.

John Grisham's Success Story: From Lawyer to Bestselling Author

"A great book launch is the author's chance to make a powerful first impression; it sets the tone for the sales trajectory and builds essential momentum that can turn a new title into a must-read." — JOHN GRISHAM, BESTSELLING AUTHOR

John Grisham is a bestselling author known for his mastery of legal thrillers. His quote, *"A great book launch is the author's chance to make a powerful first impression; it sets the tone for the sales trajectory and builds essential momentum that can turn a new title into a must-read,"* reflects his understanding of marketing strategy and the importance of a strong debut in the publishing world.

Career Beginnings: From Courtrooms to Creative Writing

Grisham began his career as a lawyer in Mississippi, where he developed a deep understanding of the legal system. During his time in courtrooms, he became inspired to write legal thrillers, blending his knowledge of the law with gripping storytelling. In the late 1980s, Grisham wrote "A Time to Kill," his debut novel, based on a trial he witnessed. Although the book initially struggled to find success, his persistence in marketing it laid the groundwork for his future breakthroughs.

Breakthrough Success with "The Firm"

Grisham's major breakthrough came in 1991 with the release of "The Firm," which became an instant bestseller. The novel's success attracted Hollywood's attention, and it was adapted into a hit film starring Tom Cruise. This launched Grisham's career to new heights, turning him into one of the most sought-after authors in the legal thriller genre.

Philosophy: The Power of a Strategic Book Launch

Grisham's quote underscores his belief in the importance of a powerful book launch. He emphasizes that the momentum created during a release is essential for long-term sales success, transforming new titles into must-read books. Grisham's approach involves strategically timed releases, engaging marketing campaigns, and media coverage, ensuring each book captures public interest from day one.

Legacy: A Literary Icon with Global Influence

Today, John Grisham is recognized as one of the world's most successful authors, with over 40 novels and hundreds of millions of copies sold worldwide. His books have not only captivated readers but also redefined the legal thriller genre. Grisham's dedication to storytelling and strategic book launches continues to serve as an inspiration to aspiring writers looking to achieve commercial success while leaving a lasting literary legacy.

Ken Burns' Success Story: Mastering Storytelling through Documentary Film

"Understanding fair use is like learning the rules of chess—you need to know how each piece moves to play the game effectively. It's about making informed choices in the creative process."

— KEN BURNS, DOCUMENTARY FILMMAKER

Ken Burns is an acclaimed documentary filmmaker, celebrated for his meticulous approach to history and storytelling. Known for his quote, *"Understanding fair use is like learning the rules of chess—you need to know how each piece moves to play the game effectively. It's about making informed choices in the creative process,"* Burns emphasizes the importance of fair use in documentary filmmaking, navigating copyright with precision to tell authentic and engaging stories.

Career Beginnings: Discovering a Passion for History and Film

Burns' interest in filmmaking began during his time at Hampshire College, where he studied documentary film. Inspired by his love of history, he realized that film could bring historical events to life in a way that captivated audiences emotionally. After college, Burns founded Florentine Films, where he began producing documentaries focusing on the American experience. His early works, though small in scale, demonstrated his unique ability to blend archival footage, narration, music, and interviews.

Breakthrough with *The Civil War*

Burns achieved widespread success with his landmark documentary "The Civil War" in 1990. This nine-part series became an unexpected cultural phenomenon, drawing millions of viewers and earning critical acclaim. The documentary's distinctive storytelling style, with moving imagery, voiceovers, and historical letters narrated by renowned actors, established what is now known as the "Ken Burns effect"—a technique that animates still photographs through slow panning and zooming.

Navigating Copyright and Fair Use

Burns' quote reflects his expertise in navigating fair use laws, which allow filmmakers to use copyrighted material under specific conditions. His meticulous

184

approach ensures that archival footage, photographs, and music are used legally and ethically, enabling him to tell complex historical stories while avoiding legal hurdles. For Burns, understanding copyright is essential to the creative process, allowing him to balance artistic expression with legal responsibility.

Legacy: A Filmmaker Shaping American Memory

Ken Burns' documentaries, including "The Civil War," "Baseball," and "Jazz," have redefined how history is told through film, inspiring audiences worldwide. His commitment to historical accuracy, emotional storytelling, and creative integrity has earned him numerous awards and made him one of the most influential filmmakers of his generation. Burns continues to explore new subjects, ensuring that America's stories are preserved for future generations.

Robert Orben's Success Story: Crafting Wit and Wisdom Through Comedy

"Time flies. It's up to you to be the navigator." — ROBERT ORBEN, AMERICAN PROFESSIONAL COMEDY WRITER

Robert Orben is an American professional comedy writer and renowned speechwriter, celebrated for his sharp wit and timeless humor. Known for his quote, *"Time flies. It's up to you to be the navigator,"* Orben's career reflects his belief in seizing moments with purpose and humor.

Early Career: From Magic to Comedy Writing

Orben's journey began with a passion for magic, publishing joke books for magicians to liven their performances. His unique comedic style quickly gained attention, leading him to become one of the most sought-after comedy writers in show business. In the 1950s and 60s, Orben wrote material for television programs, stand-up comedians, and entertainers, developing a reputation for delivering punchlines with precision and impact.

Breakthrough: Comedy Meets Politics

Beyond entertainment, Orben's talents led him to the White House, where he became a speechwriter for President Gerald Ford. His humor infused presidential speeches with levity and relatability, proving that wit can be both entertaining and politically effective. Orben's work demonstrated how comedy could engage diverse audiences, whether on a stage or in the public sphere.

Philosophy: Humor as Navigation

Orben's quote reflects his philosophy of life—that while time moves quickly, it's up to individuals to steer their course with intention and humor. His work shows that well-timed wit can make even the most complex subjects more accessible and memorable. Orben encourages others to embrace humor not just as a tool for entertainment but as a way to navigate life's challenges gracefully.

Legacy: A Lifelong Influence on Comedy and Speechwriting

Robert Orben's contributions to comedy and speechwriting continue to inspire performers, writers, and public speakers. His ability to distill wisdom into humor has made his quotes and jokes timeless classics. Whether in the entertainment industry or the political arena, Orben's work reminds us that humor can be a powerful tool to connect, inspire, and lead.

Sheri Dew's Success Story: Leading with Influence and Purpose

"Influence is not about elevating self, but about lifting others."
— SHERI DEW, AUTHOR AND BUSINESSWOMAN

Sheri Dew is an author, speaker, and businesswoman, recognized for her inspiring leadership and emphasis on empowerment through service. Known for her quote, *"Influence is not about elevating self, but about lifting others,"* Dew's success lies in her commitment to meaningful leadership, focusing on helping others grow and making a positive impact.

Early Career: Rising through Leadership Roles

Dew began her career in publishing, where she quickly rose to leadership positions due to her sharp business acumen and communication skills. In 2002, she became the CEO of Deseret Book, a role that allowed her to influence and inspire others through books, public speaking, and strategic leadership.

Philosophy: Empowering Others through Influence
Dew's leadership philosophy focuses on using influence to uplift others, demonstrating that true leadership is service-oriented. Whether writing books, mentoring professionals, or delivering keynote addresses, Dew emphasizes the importance of humility and purpose in leadership. Her belief that impactful leaders prioritize the success of those they serve has resonated across industries.

Impact and Legacy: A Voice for Values-Based Leadership
In addition to her success as an author and businesswoman, Dew is a prominent motivational speaker, delivering messages on faith, leadership, and personal growth. Her books and speeches inspire individuals to lead with integrity and purpose, fostering environments where others can thrive. Dew's career reflects her dedication to uplifting communities and organizations, leaving a legacy that empowers future leaders to influence through service.

Elizabeth Bennett's Success Story: Guiding Authors to Literary Success

"Book reviews are the lifeblood of literary success; each one acts not just as feedback but as a beacon, guiding new readers to discover your work."
— ELIZABETH BENNETT, LITERARY CONSULTANT

Elizabeth Bennett is a literary consultant renowned for her expertise in book marketing, review strategies, and reader engagement. Known for her insightful quote, *"Book reviews are the lifeblood of literary success; each one acts not just as feedback but as a beacon, guiding new readers to discover your work,"* Bennett emphasizes the crucial role of book reviews not only in building credibility but also in driving visibility and long-term success for authors.

Early Career: From Publishing Professional to Literary Consultant
Bennett's career began in traditional publishing, where she worked closely with authors, editors, and marketers to develop book launch campaigns. In these early roles, she quickly realized that while marketing strategies were evolving, many authors struggled to secure and utilize effective book reviews. Recognizing a need

for better guidance, Bennett transitioned from publishing to consulting, where she could focus entirely on strategic review management—helping authors build a robust network of reviewers to boost their books' presence and influence.

Philosophy: Reviews as Marketing Beacons and Conversations

Bennett's approach to book reviews is rooted in the idea that they serve as vital connections between authors and potential readers. For her, each review is more than feedback—it's a marker of credibility that amplifies a book's reach. Reviews, in her view, are beacons of guidance, leading readers to discover works they might otherwise miss. Bennett advises authors to engage with reviewers thoughtfully, fostering authentic conversations that go beyond star ratings and summaries. She teaches that by building relationships with reviewers, authors create lasting ripple effects in the literary community.

Crafting a Strategic Review Campaign

Through her consulting work, Bennett designs tailored review campaigns for authors, emphasizing timing, platform targeting, and authenticity. She stresses that reviews on platforms like Amazon and Goodreads must come early in the book's life cycle to generate momentum and sustained visibility. Bennett also helps authors cultivate influential reviewers and book bloggers to ensure a steady stream of meaningful reviews throughout a title's release and beyond.

Her strategies extend beyond simply collecting reviews—Bennett teaches authors how to leverage positive reviews in social media campaigns, newsletters, and book blurbs, turning them into powerful marketing tools. For her, the success of a book isn't just about launching well but about creating ongoing conversations that keep readers engaged.

Navigating Challenges: Building Resilience in a Competitive Market

Bennett knows that the publishing landscape can be daunting for authors, especially those navigating the competitive self-publishing market. She helps clients overcome the fear of negative reviews by framing criticism as valuable insights for future projects. Bennett's expertise lies not only in managing positive feedback but also in turning constructive criticism into actionable advice that helps authors grow.

Her resilience-focused approach ensures that authors stay motivated and maintain a long-term vision for their books, even when faced with challenges like delayed feedback or tough reviews. This attitude has made her a sought-after consultant for authors looking to sustain momentum and thrive in an ever-changing industry.

Legacy: Shaping the Future of Literary Success

Elizabeth Bennett's influence extends across the literary world, where she has worked with emerging and established authors alike. Her approach has helped many authors achieve commercial and critical success, making reviews a cornerstone of their marketing efforts. She has also led workshops and speaking engagements, sharing her knowledge on review strategies, reader engagement, and book marketing with audiences worldwide.

Her philosophy that book reviews guide readers and shape success has set new standards in the industry, encouraging authors to embrace reviews as part of the creative process. Through her consulting work, Bennett continues to inspire authors to approach the literary journey with confidence, ensuring that every book, no matter how niche, finds its audience.

Bennett's legacy lies in her ability to empower authors to turn reviews into lasting success, making her a trusted ally in the competitive world of publishing. Her work demonstrates that with the right strategy, every book has the potential to become a must-read.

Rebecca Ford's Success Story: The Father of Modern Marketing

"Think of your book promotion as a movie trailer for your writing. It's about using cinematic flair to transform each synopsis into a visual feast that leaves readers eager to turn the page." — REBECCA FORD, MARKETING DIRECTOR AND FILM ENTHUSIAST

Rebecca Ford is a marketing director and film enthusiast known for her innovative approach to book promotion. Her quote, *"Think of your book promotion as a movie trailer for your writing. It's about using cinematic flair to transform each*

189

synopsis into a visual feast that leaves readers eager to turn the page," reflects her belief in merging cinematic storytelling with book marketing to captivate audiences.

Early Career: Merging Passion for Film and Marketing

Ford's journey began with a love for both film and literature, which led her to explore creative marketing roles in publishing. Early on, she recognized that visual storytelling techniques from film could elevate how books are promoted. She focused on engaging readers through short-form promotional content, treating each book like a film trailer designed to evoke curiosity. This innovative strategy set her apart from traditional marketers.

Crafting Campaigns that Captivate

Ford's success lies in her ability to transform book summaries into cinematic experiences, ensuring that each promotion feels like an invitation to an immersive story. Whether through dynamic book trailers, engaging social media content, or visually compelling newsletters, her campaigns focus on creating anticipation and leaving potential readers eager to explore more.

Ford also emphasizes the importance of cohesive branding and storytelling across all platforms. For her, every element—from the tagline to the imagery—must work together to evoke the same emotional response that readers will find in the book itself.

Philosophy: Book Promotion as Cinematic Art

Ford's marketing philosophy revolves around using cinematic flair to engage readers emotionally. She teaches that every promotional piece should be treated like a visual work of art, focusing on evoking emotion and building anticipation. For Ford, book trailers are not just summaries—they're visual experiences that give readers a taste of the narrative's tone, setting, and intrigue.

Legacy: A Pioneer in Visual Book Marketing

Rebecca Ford's influence extends throughout the publishing world, where her pioneering approach to book marketing has redefined how stories are promoted. Her work with authors and publishers has not only increased sales but also enhanced reader engagement, helping books stand out in a crowded marketplace. Through workshops, consulting, and speaking engagements, Ford continues to inspire a new generation of marketers to think beyond traditional methods and embrace visual storytelling.

Her legacy lies in her ability to bridge the worlds of film and literature, crafting campaigns that are memorable, engaging, and effective. Rebecca Ford's work demonstrates that creative book promotion is an art form in itself, and when done right, it can transform a book into a must-read experience.

Steven Spielberg's Success Story: A Filmmaker Who Redefined Storytelling Through Cinema

"Video provides the most immediate way to connect with an audience, transcending mere words to deliver experiences that engage on every level." — STEVEN SPIELBERG, FILMMAKER

Steven Spielberg is a legendary filmmaker whose career has transformed the world of cinema with groundbreaking films that capture the imagination of audiences worldwide. Known for his quote, *"Video provides the most immediate way to connect with an audience, transcending mere words to deliver experiences that engage on every level,"* Spielberg emphasizes the immersive power of visual storytelling.

Early Life: Discovering a Passion for Filmmaking

Spielberg's journey began with a childhood love for filmmaking and storytelling. As a young boy, he made home movies with his family's camera, showcasing a natural talent for visual storytelling. His early fascination with film led him to create short films and amateur projects, laying the foundation for his future success. Despite facing initial setbacks—such as being rejected from film school—Spielberg's determination and passion for cinema never wavered.

Breaking into Hollywood: An Unstoppable Visionary

Spielberg's first major breakthrough came with "Jaws" (1975), a blockbuster that redefined suspense and became one of the highest-grossing films of all time. From there, Spielberg continued to revolutionize the film industry with masterpieces like "E.T.," "Raiders of the Lost Ark," and "Jurassic Park." His ability to blend narrative, visual effects, and emotion captivated audiences, making him one of the most influential filmmakers in history.

Philosophy: Engaging Through Visual Experiences

Spielberg's quote reflects his belief that film transcends language, engaging audiences emotionally and viscerally. For him, video storytelling is about creating experiences that connect viewers across cultures and generations. He emphasizes that visual media communicates beyond words, fostering empathy and immersion in ways other forms of art cannot.

Legacy: A Lasting Impact on the Film Industry

Throughout his career, Spielberg has directed and produced iconic films across multiple genres, earning numerous Oscars, Golden Globes, and critical acclaim. His influence extends beyond filmmaking—through his work with Amblin Entertainment and DreamWorks, Spielberg has mentored new generations of filmmakers and shaped the industry with cutting-edge storytelling techniques.

His legacy lies in his ability to create timeless stories that resonate with audiences emotionally, leaving a profound impact on film, culture, and storytelling. Spielberg's work demonstrates that cinema is more than just entertainment—it is an immersive experience that connects, inspires, and transforms.

Conclusion

Growth, Connection, and Legacy—
Building a Future That Lasts

The journey through the 74 case studies in this volume has revealed powerful lessons on how growth, digital presence, and legacy are interconnected in shaping sustainable success. Each story demonstrates that success is neither instantaneous nor accidental—it is cultivated through careful planning, resilience, and a deep understanding of what matters most. While markets evolve, technologies shift, and challenges arise, the core principles of growth, relevance, and impact remain consistent. This volume offers a blueprint for those seeking to not only grow their businesses but also build something lasting—something that will echo through generations.

The Continuous Journey of Growth

Growth is often seen as a destination, but these case studies show that it is, in fact, an ongoing process of learning, adapting, and evolving. Business expansion is not just about increasing size or profits—it is about identifying opportunities to add value, solve real-world problems, and engage meaningfully with customers.

Leaders like Ken Burns and Rebecca Ford remind us that authentic growth comes from curiosity, creativity, and strategic vision, while also recognizing the need for patience when progress feels slow.

Through successes and failures, these leaders demonstrated that setbacks are not the end of the road—they are part of the process. Many businesses reach critical points where pivoting is necessary to survive and thrive. The willingness to change direction, embrace new ideas, and reimagine the future—just as Steven Spielberg did with his filmmaking ventures—ensures that growth remains sustainable. Each chapter in this book underscores the importance of staying agile, learning from challenges, and evolving with intention.

Ultimately, the path to meaningful growth is not linear; it requires balancing short-term wins with long-term strategies. It demands setting clear goals, while remaining flexible enough to adjust plans when circumstances shift. This volume teaches us that real growth lies not only in what a business accomplishes today but in the foundations it lays for tomorrow.

Creating a Digital Presence That Resonates

The digital age has revolutionized how businesses connect with their audiences, making an online presence essential for survival and success. However, as these case studies show, merely existing in the digital space is not enough—it requires thoughtful strategy, authenticity, and consistency. Leaders like John Grisham, who adapted to the evolving landscape of digital publishing, demonstrate that the key to a strong online presence is understanding your audience's needs and meeting them where they are.

Creating a compelling digital presence involves more than using social media platforms or building websites—it requires crafting narratives that reflect the brand's identity, values, and purpose. Elizabeth Bennett's ability to use storytelling as a tool for meaningful engagement serves as a powerful reminder that technology should amplify, not replace, the human connection. Whether through blogs, podcasts, newsletters, or social media, every digital touchpoint must reflect the heart of the brand.

Furthermore, this volume highlights the importance of consistency across all channels. A cohesive digital presence builds trust with audiences, encouraging long-term engagement. Today's customers are savvy and value transparency—if a brand's messaging across platforms feels disjointed or inauthentic, it risks losing credibility. Leaders like Sheri Dew, who leveraged consistent messaging to build communities of trust, teach us that authenticity is not a trend—it is a requirement for meaningful connection.

A strong digital presence also requires adaptability. As technology evolves and trends shift, businesses must be willing to experiment with new tools and platforms while staying grounded in their core values. From SEO optimization to personalized email campaigns, each case study in this volume emphasizes the importance of integrating both strategy and creativity to remain relevant in an ever-changing digital landscape.

Leaving a Legacy That Transcends Time

Building a lasting legacy is perhaps the most profound lesson this volume offers. Legacy is not just about personal or business achievements—it is about the lasting impact we leave on the people, communities, and industries we touch. Leaders like Robert Orben and Martin Reese demonstrate that a legacy is built through ideas, values, and actions that inspire future generations to carry the mission forward.

A true legacy extends beyond financial success or market dominance. It lives in the culture, relationships, and values instilled within a business and shared with its community. Just as Steven Spielberg's body of work continues to inspire new generations of filmmakers, the businesses and leaders highlighted in these case studies have created lasting impact by aligning their work with a higher purpose.

This chapter explores how legacy is shaped not only by grand accomplishments but also by the daily decisions that define a brand's identity. Leaders like John Grisham and Sheri Dew remind us that the small, consistent actions we take—whether in business strategy, personal conduct, or community involvement—create ripples that extend far beyond our immediate sphere of influence. A legacy is not just the sum of past achievements; it is the foundation upon which others can build and grow.

This volume also emphasizes the importance of mentoring and collaboration in building a legacy. Many of the case studies reveal that true leadership involves empowering others, sharing knowledge, and fostering a culture of growth within teams and communities. As Robert Orben wisely noted, "A good speech should be like a woman's skirt; long enough to cover the subject and short enough to create interest." Similarly, a meaningful legacy is both expansive and accessible—it covers essential ground while leaving room for others to contribute, innovate, and carry the torch forward.

Integrating Growth, Digital Presence, and Legacy

The intersection of growth, digital presence, and legacy is where businesses find their most enduring success. This volume demonstrates that sustainable growth requires a deep understanding of one's digital presence and how it supports long-term goals. Leaders who master this integration build businesses that thrive not only in the present but also create a lasting impact on future generations.

In an interconnected world, every interaction—whether through digital campaigns, product launches, or customer relationships—contributes to the narrative of a business's legacy. The case studies in this volume highlight the importance of thinking beyond immediate results and focusing on the bigger picture: How does this business contribute to the community? How will it be remembered? What values will endure long after the founder steps away?

The ability to balance growth with purpose, digital presence with authenticity, and ambition with legacy is what distinguishes businesses that survive from those that thrive. This book offers a road map for entrepreneurs, leaders, and creatives seeking to build enterprises that make an impact far beyond the present moment.

A Call to Action

As you close this book, the lessons learned from the leaders and businesses featured here now rest in your hands. Growth is not a destination but a continuous journey of exploration and learning. A digital presence is not just about being seen but about building connections that matter. And legacy is not reserved for the famous or the powerful—it is within reach of anyone willing to leave the world better than they found it.

Your story is still being written. How will you grow your business with purpose? How will you engage with your audience in a way that resonates and inspires?

And most importantly, what legacy will you leave for those who follow in your footsteps?

Whether you are just starting your entrepreneurial journey or refining an established brand, the insights from these case studies will guide you in building a future that aligns with your values and aspirations. The path ahead may not always be clear, but with purpose, resilience, and intention, you can create something truly extraordinary—something that lasts.

The time to act is now. Build boldly, connect authentically, and leave a legacy that matters. The world is waiting for what only you can create.

Resources

The Empire Builders and Blueprint Series

Welcome to the Resource section of the Empire Builders Series: Masterclasses in Business and Law. Here, we provide a carefully curated collection of practical tools and materials designed to complement the strategies and insights discussed throughout the series. This section is your gateway to deeper understanding and application, offering everything from sample agreements and checklists to detailed case studies and guidelines. Whether you're forging a new business, protecting intellectual property, or planning for expansion, these resources are intended to empower you with the necessary tools to effectively implement and navigate the complex landscape of business and law. Embrace these resources as your companion in building and sustaining a robust empire.

Empire Builders Series:
Masterclasses in Business and Law

In the dynamic world of business, where innovation intersects with opportunity, success often hinges not only on creativity but also on a deep understanding of the legal and operational landscapes. The Empire Builders Series is meticulously designed to arm aspiring entrepreneurs, seasoned business owners, creative professionals, and legal experts with the comprehensive knowledge and strategies needed to navigate these complexities and build lasting empires.

Each book in the series serves as a foundational pillar, offering expert guidance and actionable insights in specific areas of business and law; tailored to foster growth, innovation, and success in today's competitive marketplace:

1. **Brick by Brick**: This guide acts as your blueprint for building a business from the ground up. It offers essential strategies, legal insights, and operational tactics crucial for establishing a solid foundation for any business venture.

2. **Mark Your Territory**: Dive deep into the world of trademarks with this essential guide, designed to help you protect and effectively leverage your brand in today's competitive market.

3. **From Idea to Empire**: Transform your entrepreneurial dreams into reality with this exhaustive guide to business planning. Learn how to craft a compelling business plan that not only attracts investors but also sets the stage for a successful enterprise.

4. **Beyond the Pen**: Safeguard your creative works and master the intricacies of copyright law with this expert guide, tailored specifically for writers, artists, musicians, and digital content creators.

5. **Legal Ink**: Demystify the complex legal landscape of publishing with practical advice on negotiating contracts and protecting intellectual property, essential for authors and publishers.

The Empire Builders Series stands as a testament to the power of knowledge and the importance of mastering the strategic and legal aspects of business management. Each book is designed not merely to inform but to inspire action and lead to success. Embark on this journey to build your empire, one masterclass at a time.

Brick by Brick:
The Entrepreneur's Guide to Constructing a Company

The first book in the Empire Builders Series: Masterclass in Business and Law is "Brick by Brick: The Entrepreneur's Guide to Constructing a Company."

Summary: "Brick by Brick" is an indispensable resource for entrepreneurs who are poised to transform their innovative business ideas into successful enterprises. This comprehensive guide meticulously outlines the complexities of business formation, providing detailed, step-by-step instructions and vital insights into the legal, operational, and strategic aspects of starting and running a thriving company.

Part 1: Laying the Foundation – Focuses on selecting the appropriate business entity, delving into the legal implications of each option and the economic considerations vital for establishing a solid foundation for your business.

Part 2: Operational Mechanics – Discusses the operational aspects of setting up partnerships and LLCs, navigating corporate governance, maintaining corporate records, and managing capital and shareholder relationships effectively.

Part 3: Advanced Strategic Planning – Offers insights into managing structural changes, handling stock and ownership issues, expanding operations across state lines, and deploying tax strategies to ensure compliance and optimize financial performance.

Part 4: Implementation Tools and Resources – Provides practical tools such as sample agreements, startup task checklists, and comprehensive guidelines for drafting business plans and the incorporation process, enabling entrepreneurs to effectively implement their business strategies.

"Brick by Brick" not only serves as a guide but acts as a complete blueprint for building a robust business capable of thriving in today's competitive market. It arms aspiring entrepreneurs with the necessary knowledge and tools to navigate the complexities of business formation. From drafting your first business plan to preparing for incorporation, this book delivers invaluable insights and practical advice to establish a strong foundation and sustain growth.

Mark Your Territory:
Navigating Trademarks in the Modern Marketplace

The second book in the Empire Builders Series: Masterclass in Business and Law is "Mark Your Territory: Navigating Trademarks in the Modern Marketplace."

Summary: "Mark Your Territory" provides an indispensable resource for anyone involved in the branding and legal aspects of their business, offering a comprehensive guide to understanding, acquiring, and effectively managing trademarks. This book is crucial for ensuring that trademarks, which are vital assets to any business, are properly protected and leveraged.

Part 1: Fundamentals of Trademarks – Introduces the basics of trademarks, including their legal framework, the process of trademark selection and registration, and their importance in identifying business sources and ensuring product quality.

Part 2: Strategic Trademark Management – Focuses on the ongoing management of trademarks, detailing strategies for maintaining rights, monitoring for infringements, addressing challenges in digital marketing, and managing global trademark portfolios.

Part 3: Advanced Topics in Trademarks – Delves into more complex issues such as preventing trademark dilution, managing renewals, understanding the specific needs of service marks in advertising, and navigating the intricacies of trademark licensing and emerging legal trends.

Part 4: Practical Tools and Resources – Provides practical aids like sample trademark filings, management checklists, and insightful case studies, equipping readers with tangible tools and real-world examples to apply the concepts discussed effectively.

Designed for entrepreneurs, business owners, and legal professionals, "Mark Your Territory" equips readers with actionable strategies and essential tools for effective trademark management. It ensures that readers can maintain their brand's uniqueness and legal protections, thus securing a competitive edge in the marketplace.

From Idea to Empire:
Mastering the Art of Business Planning

The third book in the Empire Builders Series: Masterclass in Business and Law is "From Idea to Empire: Mastering the Art of Business Planning."

Summary: "From Idea to Empire" offers an indispensable roadmap for entrepreneurs eager to transform their innovative ideas into successful businesses. This comprehensive guide equips readers with a strategic blueprint for drafting robust business plans that attract investors and serve as a roadmap for navigating the transition from startup to thriving enterprise.

Part 1: Conceptualizing Your Business – This section lays the groundwork by assisting readers in defining their business vision, understanding market needs, analyzing competitors, and setting clear business objectives. It also guides readers in selecting an effective business model that aligns with their long-term goals.

Part 2: Strategic Planning – Delve into creating detailed marketing strategies, operational plans, and financial projections. This part covers risk management and technological integration, ensuring the business plan is both innovative and executable.

Part 3: Articulating Your Plan – Focuses on the actual drafting of the business plan, including how to write an engaging executive summary, develop compelling proposals, and master communication and negotiation tactics with potential investors and partners.

Part 4: Execution and Review – Outlines the necessary steps to launch the business successfully, monitor its performance, and make adjustments based on real-world feedback and market dynamics. This section also explores strategies for sustainable growth and long-term viability.

"From Idea to Empire" is more than a mere planning manual; it's a strategic guide that provides budding entrepreneurs with the necessary knowledge, tools, and confidence to build a business capable of facing today's market complexities. With practical advice, real-world examples, and essential resources, this book is a vital tool for anyone ready to evolve their business concept from idea to a profitable empire.

From Idea to Empire: Abridged Edition

The third book in the Empire Builders Series: Masterclass in Business and Law is "From Idea to Empire: Abridged Edition."

Summary: "From Idea to Empire: Abridged Edition" delivers the essential roadmap for turning business ideas into successful enterprises—streamlined for readers seeking concise and actionable insights. While the original edition provides an expansive resource with success stories and detailed case studies, this abridged version focuses solely on the strategic elements of business planning, offering the tools needed to conceptualize, design, and execute a winning business strategy.

By eliminating supplementary stories and focusing on the practical frameworks, this edition is perfect for readers eager to dive straight into the mechanics of business planning without distraction. It provides the knowledge required to develop robust business models, articulate compelling proposals, and successfully launch and grow a business in today's dynamic marketplace.

Part 1: Conceptualizing Your Business – Laying the Foundation – In this section, readers learn how to define their business idea, identify market needs, analyze competitors, and set clear objectives. It introduces essential business models and helps entrepreneurs align their vision with long-term goals.

Part 2: Strategic Planning – Mapping the Path to Success – Here, readers will discover how to design effective marketing strategies, operational plans, and financial projections. Topics like risk management and technological integration are covered to ensure every business plan is both realistic and innovative.

Part 3: Articulating Your Plan – Communicating with Precision and Impact – This section emphasizes the importance of clarity in communication. Readers will learn how to craft compelling executive summaries, develop strong proposals, and master negotiation strategies for working with investors and partners.

Part 4: Execution and Review – Launching and Scaling with Purpose – The final section covers essential steps for launching a business successfully, monitoring performance, and making real-time adjustments. It also addresses strategies for sustainable growth, long-term resilience, and market adaptation.

About This Edition:
The Abridged Edition is crafted for readers who prefer a focused, no-frills approach to business planning. By presenting the core methodologies from the original book in a concise format, this version allows entrepreneurs to absorb key concepts quickly and efficiently. Whether you're a first-time entrepreneur or a seasoned business owner, this streamlined guide provides the essential tools needed to transform an idea into a thriving business.

Why This Edition Matters:
"From Idea to Empire: Abridged Edition" underscores that great business planning doesn't require lengthy explanations—it requires clear strategies and actionable frameworks. This edition emphasizes the importance of focus, discipline, and adaptability in building a successful business.

Designed to complement busy entrepreneurs, it delivers the same powerful strategies as the original book but in a more accessible format. Readers can quickly refer to specific sections, apply the knowledge, and move forward with confidence in their business endeavors.

"From Idea to Empire: Abridged Edition" is the perfect companion for entrepreneurs who need to move swiftly from concept to execution. With straightforward advice and practical insights, this edition equips readers to create robust business plans and take decisive action toward building their own empire.

Beyond the Pen:
Copyright Strategies for Modern Creators
The fourth book in the Empire Builders Series: Masterclass in Business and Law is "Beyond the Pen: Copyright Strategies for Modern Creators."

Summary: "Beyond the Pen" serves as a crucial guide for artists, writers, musicians, and digital creators who seek to effectively navigate the complexities of copyright law and protect their creative assets. This comprehensive resource provides a deep dive into the mechanisms, legal frameworks, and strategic practices necessary to safeguard intellectual property in today's rapidly evolving digital landscape.

Part 1: Understanding Copyright Law – This section lays the groundwork by covering the essentials of copyright, including how to register works, the extent of legal protection available, and the nuances of international copyright laws. It equips creators with the crucial knowledge needed to assert and defend their rights.

Part 2: Navigating Use and Fair Use – Focuses on the vital concept of fair use, offering real-world scenarios and detailed guidance on how to handle copyright infringements and resolve disputes effectively without compromising creative freedom.

Part 3: Licensing and Monetization – Explores strategic approaches to structuring and managing licensing agreements, understanding diverse revenue models, and handling collaborations, ensuring creators can monetize their works effectively while maintaining control over their usage.

Part 4: Copyright in the Digital Age – Addresses the challenges and opportunities presented by new technologies, digital rights management, and online content sharing platforms. This part also examines the impact of social media on copyright and anticipates future trends that could influence creators' rights.

"Beyond the Pen" is more than just a legal manual; it is a strategic resource that empowers creators to protect, manage, and prosper with their intellectual property in today's interconnected market. Packed with practical examples, expert advice, and actionable strategies, this book is an indispensable tool for anyone looking to navigate the legal challenges and seize the opportunities in the modern creative landscape.

Legal Ink:
Navigating the Legalese of Publishing

The fifth book in the Empire Builders Series: Masterclass in Business and Law is "Legal Ink: Navigating the Legalese of Publishing."

Summary: "Legal Ink" offers an indispensable guide for authors seeking to navigate the complex world of publishing contracts. This comprehensive book demystifies legal jargon and provides a clear roadmap to understanding and managing the intricacies of publishing agreements effectively.

Part 1: The Grant of Rights – This section explains the various types of publishing rights, offering guidance on how to negotiate and manage these rights effectively to safeguard the author's interests.

Part 2: Your Obligations – Details the commitments authors must uphold under publishing contracts. It emphasizes the implications of these obligations for an author's literary career and advises on managing multiple contractual commitments.

Part 3: Getting Your Book to Market – Covers the practical aspects of the publishing process from the final manuscript preparation to marketing and distribution. This part ensures authors understand the steps involved and their roles in bringing their book to market.

Part 4: Follow the Money – Breaks down the financial components of publishing contracts, including advances, royalties, and accounting clauses. It offers crucial advice on how to negotiate for fair compensation.

Part 5: Parting Ways – Discusses strategies for effectively managing the conclusion of a publishing agreement, including rights reversion and contract termination, providing tactics for authors to regain control of their work.

"Legal Ink" acts as more than just a guide—it's a strategic tool for any author looking to deeply understand and master the legal framework of publishing contracts. With this book, writers are equipped to make informed decisions, negotiate better terms, and ensure their rights are protected throughout their publishing journey. It is an essential resource for anyone looking to confidently handle the legalities of publishing and secure the success of their work in the competitive marketplace.

The Empire Blueprint Series:
Case Studies for Business Success

Welcome to the Case Studies section of The Empire Blueprint Series: Case Studies for Business Success. This collection serves as an essential companion to the theoretical knowledge presented in the earlier volumes. Here, we delve into real-world applications and successful business practices through detailed case studies, showcasing how various entrepreneurs and businesses have navigated challenges, seized opportunities, and achieved success in their respective fields.

In this series, you will encounter a variety of scenarios that illustrate the practical implementation of business strategies and legal frameworks. Each case study not only highlights successes but also discusses the obstacles faced and lessons learned along the way. Whether you're a budding entrepreneur, a seasoned executive, or a legal professional, these insights will provide you with invaluable perspectives and tools to enhance your own business endeavors.

Each book in the series includes:

1. **70 Case Studies in Vision, Strategy, and Personal Branding**: This volume explores the journeys of entrepreneurs who have effectively crafted their visions and built strong personal brands. It highlights strategies for aligning personal values with business goals and creating a lasting impact in the marketplace.

2. **70 Case Studies in Leadership, Innovation, and Resilience**: This volume examines leaders who have driven innovation and fostered resilience within their organizations. The case studies showcase their approaches to overcoming challenges and inspire others to cultivate a culture of adaptability and forward-thinking.

3. **74 Case Studies in Growth, Digital Presence, and Legacy Building**: This volume delves into the strategies employed by businesses that have successfully navigated digital transformation and growth. It emphasizes the

importance of establishing a strong online presence and building a legacy that resonates with future generations.

Each case study in The Empire Blueprint Series: Case Studies for Business Success is crafted to offer actionable insights and inspiration for readers. By examining these real-world examples, you will gain a deeper understanding of the strategies that drive business success and how to apply these lessons to your own ventures.

70 Case Studies in Vision, Strategy, and Personal Branding: The Foundations of Success, Volume 1

The first book in The Empire Blueprint Series: Case Studies for Business Success is "70 Case Studies in Vision, Strategy, and Personal Branding: The Foundations of Success," Volume 1

Dive deeper into the essential elements of business success with Volume 1: 70 Case Studies in Vision, Strategy, and Personal Branding. This volume not only presents a wealth of real-world examples but also serves as a practical toolkit for aspiring entrepreneurs and seasoned professionals alike. Here, you will find a curated collection of resources designed to complement the case studies and enhance your understanding of effective business practices.

From strategic planning templates and personal branding frameworks to time management guides and storytelling techniques, these resources empower you to implement the insights gleaned from the case studies. Explore practical tools for optimizing your online presence, launching impactful marketing campaigns, and engaging audiences across various platforms.

With a focus on innovation and adaptability, this resource section is your go-to companion for navigating the complexities of today's business landscape. Whether you're looking to craft an inspiring vision, develop effective strategies, or build a standout personal brand, the materials provided will equip you with the actionable insights needed to achieve meaningful success. Embrace the tools and inspiration within these pages, and take your entrepreneurial journey to new heights.

70 Case Studies in Leadership, Innovation, and Resilience: Building a Thriving Enterprise, Volume 2

The second book in The Empire Blueprint Series: Case Studies for Business Success is "70 Case Studies in Leadership, Innovation, and Resilience: Building a Thriving Enterprise," Volume 2

Enhance your understanding of effective leadership with Volume 2: 70 Case Studies in Leadership, Innovation, and Resilience: Building a Thriving Enterprise. This resource section is designed to complement the rich insights presented throughout the volume, providing you with practical tools and frameworks to elevate your leadership journey.

Within this section, you'll find a variety of resources that address the core themes of this book—leadership, innovation, and resilience. From templates for developing effective communication strategies to guides on fostering a collaborative corporate culture, these materials are crafted to support your growth as a leader. Explore negotiation techniques, emotional intelligence assessments, and frameworks for ethical leadership that will help you build trust and loyalty within your teams.

The resources also include practical tips for embracing digital transformation and integrating innovative technologies into your business practices. Learn how to leverage these tools to drive growth, enhance customer engagement, and maintain a competitive edge in today's dynamic market.

With a focus on creating lasting value and building a legacy, this section equips you with actionable insights and strategies to navigate challenges with confidence. Whether you are an entrepreneur launching a new venture or an executive steering an established enterprise, these resources will empower you to lead with purpose and resilience.

Dive into these valuable tools and insights, and discover how to turn challenges into opportunities, fostering an environment where innovation and sustainable growth thrive.

74 Case Studies in Growth, Digital Presence, and Legacy Building: Strategies for Long-Term Success, Volume 3

The third book in The Empire Blueprint Series: Case Studies for Business Success is "74 Case Studies in Growth, Digital Presence, and Legacy Building: Strategies for Long-Term Success," Volume 3

Unlock the secrets to sustainable success with Volume 3: 74 Case Studies in Growth, Digital Presence, and Legacy Building: Strategies for Long-Term Success. This resource section is designed to enhance your understanding and application of the powerful insights shared throughout the volume, providing you with practical tools and strategies for thriving in today's competitive landscape.

In this section, you'll find a wealth of resources that align with the key themes of this book—growth, digital engagement, and legacy building. From templates for strategic goal-setting and growth frameworks to guides on optimizing digital marketing efforts, these materials will help you implement the actionable insights gained from the case studies.

Explore best practices for storytelling and community engagement in the digital realm, along with practical tips for leveraging social media to amplify your brand's presence. Discover frameworks for navigating the complexities of innovation and operational efficiency, ensuring your business not only grows but flourishes sustainably.

The resource section also emphasizes the importance of legacy building, offering tools for effective succession planning and community involvement. Learn how to align your everyday decisions with your long-term vision, ensuring that your enterprise leaves a lasting impact for future generations.

Whether you are an entrepreneur embarking on a new venture, an executive scaling operations, or a professional seeking to elevate your digital presence, these resources will empower you to lead with purpose and confidence. Dive into the practical tools and insights provided here, and equip yourself to navigate challenges, innovate boldly, and create a meaningful legacy.

In conclusion, the Resource section of the Empire Builders Series and Empire Blueprint Series serves as valuable extensions of the learning journey you've embarked upon. By utilizing these carefully chosen tools and materials, you are better equipped to apply the principles and strategies discussed in the series to real-world scenarios. Each resource has been tailored to enhance your understanding and effectiveness in the realms of business and law, ensuring you have the practical support necessary to navigate challenges and seize opportunities. We hope these resources prove instrumental in helping you build and sustain your business empire, transforming knowledge into actionable success.

L. A. Moeszinger also known as simply "L" is the face behind the AuthorsDoor Leadership Program: AuthorsDoor Series: *Publisher & Her World*, AuthorsDoor Advanced Series: *Publisher & Her World*, and AuthorsDoor Masterclass Series: *Publisher & Her World*. The program comprises, books, courses, and workbooks. The courses expand upon the books. The workbooks go into further detail, outlining step-by-step instructions. Courses are *free*; books and workbooks are available for purchase on Amazon and other retailer sites. She has been launching the careers of self-publishers since 2009, and she also writes the AuthorsRedDoor.com blog on writing, publishing, and marketing. L is also the co-founder of The Ridge Publishing Group and its imprints.

She is an American author, publisher, and creator who resides in Coeur d'Alene, Idaho, with her husband and two dogs. She writes under the pseudonyms: Ann Patterson and Ann Carrington for her business law pieces; L. A. Moeszinger for her writing, publishing, and marketing pieces; Lori Ann Moeszinger for her biblical books and personal pieces; and a handful of others for her Manhattan Diaries series. She believes strongly in faith, blessings, and working her butt off . . . and she thinks one of the best things about being an author-publisher—unlike the lawyer she used to be—is that she can let her passion out.

Original Package Design
© 2024 AuthorsDoor Leadership Program
Cover Design: Eric Moeszinger
Author Photo © 2023 Edwin Wolfe

Parent Website: https://www.RidgePublishingGroup.com and

blog site https://www.PublisherAndHerWorld.com

Publisher Website: https://www.GuardiansofBiblicalTruth.com and

blog site https://www.Jesus-Says.com

Author website: https://www.LAMoeszinger.com and New Youniversity sites:

https://www.NewYouniversity.com, https://www.ManhattanChronicles.com

Bridge Website: https://www.AuthorsDoor.com and

blog site https://www.AuthorsRedDoor.com

Entertainment website: https://www.EthanFoxBooks.com and

blog site https://www.KidsStagram.com

Want More?

The ideas in this book are expanded upon throughout the AuthorsDoor Leadership Program of books, courses, and workbooks. Follow our Facebook page. Join our Facebook private group. Watch our YouTube channels (AuthorsDoor Group, Authors Red Door #Shorts, and Publisher and Her World at Ridge Publishing Group). Listen to our Podcast channel (Publisher's Circle); or email me: *Hello@AuthorsDoor.com*

AuthorsDoor Hubs

Get insights from the articles we write on our *website* (AuthorsDoor.com). You'll find more publications to help authors sell better, pitch better, recruit better, build better, create better, and connect better. You are also invited to visit our *blog* and find out what we're talking about now. Sign up for our *AuthorsDoor Leadership Program Newsletter* and join the conversations going on there with our private community (Publisher's Circle); visit: *www.AuthorsRedDoor.com*

Publisher & Her World Blogs

Enter a world where the sometimes shocking and often hilarious climb to the top as an author-publisher is exposed by a true insider. Faced with on-going trials and tribulations of the world of self-publishing, L. A. Moeszinger is witty and sometimes brutally candid in her postings. If you enjoy getting the inside scoop on the makings and thoughts behind self-publishing, this is the blog for you! *www.PublisherAndHerWorld.com*

This

book was art

directed by John Jared.

The art for both the cover and the

interior was created using pastels on toned

print making paper. The text was set in 10 point Times

New Roman, a typeface based on the sixteenth-century type designs

of Claude Garamond, redrawn by Robert Slimback in 1989.

The book was printed at Amazon and IngramSpark.

The Managing Editor was Jack Clark. The

Production was supervised by

Jason Reed and Ed

Warren.